QUANTUM FASTING

FOOD FOR THOUGHT

L. Emerson Ferrell

Ana Méndez Ferrell, Inc.

Thoughts From the Artist About the Cover

For as long I am able to remember a female statue, appearing as omnipresent lights the pathways of the city dwellers. She is called "great freedom" and her light offers us orientation on our paths. Even though the place at which I stand feels limitless, I sense limitations and boundaries and know there must be more.

One day I realized, that I am standing on a pedestal hewn of stone and writen under me is the inscription, "Introite, nam et heic Dii sunt" (Come in, cause there are gods here as well) I neither know what the inscription means nor am I clear about why I am on the pedestal but it has become the foundation for my thinking. My unyielding, rigid and firm senses resemble the pedestal that has become my foundation. I become strong by my own strength.

Since Jesus touched me I have tried sincerely and entirely to trust Him completely with my whole heart. Even though He lives in me it feels most times as though He is far away. Sometimes I see His glory like a shooting star, which enters my earthly conscience just to fade away within seconds. I do believe based on knowledge. But that is not enough for me anymore. My desperate cries are bouncing off a glass wall, back to me. It's a crystal clear wall, almost invisible. I long so much to flee the urban desert. My heart is longing for a limitless life.

At that very moment I heard His voice deep in my heart: "Eat!" Completely puzzled I ask myself eat what? The voice responds loudly, "Eat of me." Suddenly, everything vibrates and shakes followed by a warm, intense sparkling light hovering in my hand. It is fresh and alive – hidden manna. I start to eat. Then I hear a faint cracking sound. Something begins to break. The energy - laden atmosphere is starting to rip. Crystals are rubbing against each other. In a loud explosion the crystal glass wall bursts into pieces in front of my eyes. Instantly, a fresh cool breeze rushes inside my mind and body expanding my horizons. Free and outside of time I step into a familiar, still unknown world. Words being able to describe this cannot follow me any longer. I am at the place where my God dwells – I am home.

We would have healed Babylon, but she cannot be healed ... (Jeremiah 51,9 german translation)

Joel Argast

QUANTUM FASTING

FOOD FOR THOUGHT

L. Emerson Ferrell

QUANTUM FASTING - FOOD FOR THOUGHT

1ST Edition, Copyright © 2012 L. Emerson Ferrell.

All Scripture quotations, are taken from the following Sources
Amplified Bible Version 1.1 (AMP) © 1954, 1958, 1962, 1964, 1965, 1987 by The Lockman Foundation, La Habra, CA 90631. All rights reserved. www.lockman.org
New American Standard Bible, 1995 edition, with Strong's numbers ©1960, 1962, 1963, 1968, 1971, 1972, 1973, 1975, 1977, 1995 by The Lockman Foundation. All rights reserved
King James Version with Strong's Numbers, in Public Domain
American Standard Version of 1901, in Public Domain
Bible in Basic English (BBE, 1965), in Public Domain. Cambridge Press in England printed the Bible In Basic English in 1965. Published without any copyright notice and distributed in America, this work fell immediately and irretrievably into the Public Domain in the United States according to the UCC convention of that time.
J.N. Darby, The 'Holy Scriptures': A New Translation from the Original Languages, in Public Domain
World English Bible (WEB) - "World English Bible" is a trademark of Rainbow Missions, Inc. Permission is granted to use the name "World English Bible" and its logo only to identify faithful copies of the Public Domain translation of the Holy Bible of that name published by Rainbow Missions, Inc. The World English Bible is not copyrighted.
Weymouth New Testament in Modern Speech (1913), in Public Domain
Young's Literal Translation of the Holy Bible, in Public Domain
The NET Bible®, First Edition, The Translation That Explains Itself™ © 1996-2005 by Biblical Studies Press, L.L.C. All Rights Reserved
GOD'S WORD® Translation, ©1995 God's Word to the Nations All rights reserved, Published by: Green Key Books, 2514 Aloha Place, Holiday, Florida 34691
New Revised Standard Version of the Bible, The Scripture quotations contained herein are from the New Revised Standard Version of the Bible, copyrighted, 1989 by the Division of Christian Education of the National Council of the Churches of Christ in the United States of America, and are used by permission. All rights reserved.
The Holy Bible, by Noah Webster, LL. D. (1833), in Public Domain.
Contemporary English Version® Copyright © 1995 American Bible Society.
Holman Christian Standard Bible®, Copyright © 1999, 2000, 2002, 2003, 2009 by Holman Bible Publishers. Used by permission. Holman Christian Standard Bible®, Holman CSB®, and HCSB® are federally registered trademarks of Holman Bible Publishers.
The Message is quoted: "Scripture taken from The Message. Copyright © 1993, 1994, 1995, 1996, 2000, 2001, 2002. Used by permission of NavPress Publishing Group."
NKJV Copyright © 1982 by Thomas Nelson, Inc.
NET Copyright © 1996-2009 by Biblical Studies Press (BSP), L.L.C. and the authors.
SB TheSchocken Guide to Jewish Books. New York: Schocken Books. 1992.
TEV completed in 1976, was translated by Robert G. Bratcher with six other scholars

Publisher:

Ana Méndez Ferrell, Inc.
P. O. Box 141, Ponte Vedra,
Florida 32004-0141.
United States of America.
www.AnaMendezFerrell.com
www.VoiceofTheLight.com

Printing in:

United States of America

ISBN 978-1-933163-65-9

CONTENTS

INTRODUCTION

This book will expose you to the world of reality beyond the physical. The life God designed for you is hidden inside your spirit along with a roadmap to righteousness, peace and joy.

The Bible says, *For the kingdom of God does not consist of food and drink, but righteousness, peace, and joy in the Holy Spirit* (Romans 14:17). My life changed forever the day the Holy Spirit revealed the depths of meaning to that verse.

It is my desire for each person to experience the ecstasies beyond this world that are available to those who fast. The devil knows the power of fasting, which is why he has stirred up so much fear of fasting in so many of God's people.

Fasting is not new even though it is not practiced often in the church. Perhaps this is due to preconceived ideas and religious beliefs. In any event, the devil has produced fear of committing to a lifestyle of fasting.

This book will enlighten and transform your understanding beyond fasting to the power over fear. Moreover, you will discover that you are what you believe because of your thoughts. Once you understand that food is one of the origins of thoughts, then you will understand the importance of fasting. Your spirit is hungrier than your body and, if fed properly, it will transform your eating and how you think.] Mind of Christ!

The power to observe and change your desires in the light of the Holy Spirit alters everything. You will be in charge of your thoughts, not a slave to them.

In addition, you will discover the hidden power inside our spirit to change our physical condition and health. The diets consumed by most people born in the West fulfill cravings generated from noise and stress. We will look at how the sounds of our souls are consistent with the foods we ingest, thus reproducing the perpetual cycle of sin, sickness and death.

You will understand how righteousness and peace are tangible foods of the Spirit served to those whose desires are consistent with His.

Science uses terms to describe phenomena in both the visible and invisible worlds. Fasting pushes open the door between the two worlds in order to feast on God's divine nature.

Quantum, according to most dictionaries, is a Latin word for amount. In modern understanding, it means the smallest possible discrete unit of any physical property, such as energy or matter.

Those who refrain from eating food (matter) will be fed faith (energy) by the Holy Spirit. A person's spirit will grow stronger and destroy the illusions of doubt and unbelief created by the constant diet of matter.

In other words, **feeding your faith is as simple as fasting along with worship and thanksgiving.**

The power to overcome the material world is to trust the Holy Spirit to provide your needs outside of your reasoning and beliefs. Fasting is an exercise in doing just that. If the devil knows you have made that choice, he is helpless to intimidate you. Your fear will be transformed to power once you begin to fast.

These experiences and more have been waiting for us since the foundation of the world. They are our inheritance and treasures for transforming future generations.

Fasting will awaken the overcoming spirit inside of you as well as increase your stamina and well being, which is necessary for the type of worship we were created to give to our King.

Jesus said, *"Do not be afraid I have overcome the world"* (John 16:33). If you are frightened about anything in your life, it is because you have <u>never</u> properly understood the benefits of fasting.

The power and authority over every terror in your life begins with overcoming the fear of not eating. **If you desire to attain power and authority, start reading now and do not stop until you have devoured every page of this book.**

Remember, Jesus did not begin to operate in the power, might and authority of the kingdom until he returned from fasting in the wilderness.

Do you want to follow in His steps? Begin now with putting all excuses aside and never looking back. **Your future is as bright as your trust in His power to transform you.**

Jesus demolished the works of the devil after His baptism and return from the wilderness. It was during those 40 days in the desert without food that something was activated inside His being. I believe that not eating was an important element in activating the divine blood of His Father.

My journey with fasting began after studying His wilderness experience and confrontations with the devil. Most Bible teachers agree that quoting scriptures was His defense against Satan. However, little is said about His lack of food as an ingredient in the victory.

The story of my experiences and discoveries is a work in progress written to demonstrate the power of the Holy Spirit over the obstacles of fear from the devil. Jesus destroyed the works of the devil, and each time I receive a new revelation about that, a greater level of authority is revealed in my life. This is a journey that increases my spiritual hunger over my physical appetites. Fasting was my vehicle for this miraculous journey, and my desire is that you will be encouraged to do the same after reading this book.

SECTION I

EARLY ANGELIC ENCOUNTERS

Throughout my life and at various times, God has intervened in order to awaken me to His amazing grace. I believe nearly everyone will have or has had a direct encounter with heaven during his or her lifetime. Nevertheless, the choice to pursue those visitations remains with each individual.

The accounts you are about to read are written to confirm and encourage others who have had similar experiences. These stories are a collection of dreams and visions I recall from early in life.

Furthermore, while these experiences impacted my life greatly, the choice to pursue those encounters was difficult. I discovered that each time heaven intervenes on earth, so does hell. The powers and principalities of darkness are fully aware when the Light of Christ illuminates the reality of God and His Kingdom. This describes what happens each time God commissions angels to show themselves.

The powers of darkness use their power of doubt and unbelief to draw the curtain on the reality of these experiences. Time and time again, God has touched humanity with His majestic love, only for it to be dismissed and forgotten.

Perhaps you are remembering things even now, which seemed out of the ordinary and strangely frightening. Be encouraged to get alone with the Holy Spirit and allow Him to remind you of those experiences.

Angelic visitations do not make someone special or unique. They are simply a reminder of His eternal love for man even at the risk of his rejection.

CHAPTER 1

DIVINE MEETINGS

At an early age, my dreams and visions exposed me to a world of reality outside of the traditional experiences most people receive in churches, schools or institutions.

It was during those years that I became acquainted with my spiritual nature. I discovered that my spirit was equipped to understand nonverbal languages as if it were the normal way of communication. In fact, it was these interactions that created a deep hunger in me for that world and later my pursuit to know Christ.

My earliest encounter began at school one day, when a friend told me an angel had once saved his life.

The early morning was hot and humid with puffy clouds in the sky. The grammar school playground was loud and noisy with the excitement that surrounds the beginning of a new school year. Finding a familiar face in the crowd was like discovering water in the desert.

From a distance, I identified the voice of a friend named David, who I knew from the previous year. He was one of the few classmates I had known who always seemed happy. He made good grades and was liked by other students, as well as by the teachers.

David was always smiling and seemed to go out of his way to help others adjust to situations and circumstances that were uncomfortable. One day my mother had forgotten to pack me a lunch and I had no money. David heard about my situation and brought me half of his sandwich. With a big smile on his face he said, "I hope you like peanut butter and jelly."

We became good friends and would share more than sandwiches during our times together. On one occasion David told me about a time that he and his mother were in a car accident. They were miraculously saved from sure death by what they discovered later to be an angel.

He told me about a tall man with penetrating eyes pulling his mother and him from their burning vehicle. He described an overwhelming feeling of peace and security. I sat mesmerized listening to David and asking him questions about the angel. I wanted to know every detail.

Often at recess, we would sit on the swings staring off into space. Daydreaming was our favorite pastime, because without saying a word we could travel beyond time and space into a makebelieve world full of innocent dreams and imaginations. Later we would relive our adventures together, which provided fuel for future excursions.

One day David and I were discussing our dreams and adventures, when we both noticed a figure standing by a huge oak tree in the middle of our playground. We both began to walk slowly towards this person. To our surprise, we were the only ones who noticed him.

My feet felt as though they were not touching the ground at one point, and it became difficult to determine if I was daydreaming. Suddenly, a voice called me by name and told me that my heavenly Father had chosen me for something special.

At the sound of that voice I felt a warm sense of peace and tranquility. However, the closer we moved towards this magnetic figure, the harder it was to move.

Suddenly, we found ourselves in front of this magnificent person whose clothes reflected a different color of light. The light was bright, but the beams emanating from it were, for lack of a better word, alive.

The most memorable feature about this person was his eyes. The color was indescribable and the intensity was laser-like. His countenance radiated power and gentleness simultaneously. *Jesus*

As we stood in front of this person, my mind was free of any thoughts. In other words, it was as if I had entered a different world, **a place that answered all my questions before I could ask them.** *outside of Time is in His Presence!*

Glory!

It was impossible for me to ascertain his age or his nationality. He did not communicate with his mouth but rather just stared into my eyes. The sensation reminded me of being on a roller coaster. I felt dizzy and nauseous, when suddenly a hand touched my forehead. Instantly, I felt better, and images raced through my head in what could only be described as a motion picture beginning to play in my mind.

I recognized myself in the feature film and intuitively understood it to be my life now and in the future. The experience was indescribable, because the person I was observing was not the person watching the film. It was as if my body and spirit were separated from one another.

I was watching my complete life from the crasdle to the grave. As I watched myself on the screen, I knew what my choices were before I made them.

Furthermore, I knew that making the right decisions pleased my heavenly Father, and the wrong ones hurt Him deeply. An overwhelming desire to please Him released a passion inside me that made me cry. I knew God wanted my life to be His, but the question inside my head was, Would I make the right choices in life?

Then, in a blink of an eye, the movie ended and what appeared to be a drop of water containing my life rolled out of my eye like a tear. As it rolled down my cheek a magnificent crystal vase shaped like a human heart captured it.

You number my wanderings. You put my tears into your bottle. Aren't they in your book?

Psalm 56:8 WEB

Suddenly, I heard my name called as it began to rain. The last thing I wanted was to leave this timeless euphoria. The instant my focus and gaze changed, I experienced a sensation of "slowing down." It was as if I stepped into lead- weighted boots and clothes.

The transition resembled what I imagined "quicksand" to feel like. All I knew was that the sensation was uncomfortable and constricting. Even my ability to know and understand things left me.

My mind was racing and heart pounding from the encounter. No words could describe it, but I knew something special had marked my life.

I remember seeing David out of the corner of my eye racing towards the school building. He waited for me at the door and flashed a big smile towards me before entering the classroom. The warmth from that grin left no doubt in my mind that we were experiencing emotions and feelings that words could not express.

That was my first experience with an angel but it was not the last.

Take care to keep open house: because in this way some have had angels as their guests, without being conscious of it.

Hebrews 13:2 GW

It was during that visitation that I remember feeling a strange sensation inside of my body and mind. My attitudes and appetites subtly began to change concerning my everyday life. It was the invisible world that captured my imagination.

My spirit was stirred and fear was replaced by the anticipation of more visitations from the unseen realm. My heart was on fire with the hope of meeting my heavenly Father.

Even at that early age, I knew my spirit was marked. I knew that the physical person was not the one who would make the choices in life, but the one who had been marked by God. It was my spirit that possessed the qualities and knowledge that I wanted to uncover.

CHAPTER 2

CHALLENGED BY HEAVEN

Several years later something happened that provided a door to that invisible world. One night while I was sitting up in my bed, I observed a heavenly being in my bedroom with a bowl in his hand. Watching intensely, I heard a voice inside my spirit ask if I wanted to taste the liquid inside the bowl.

I remember battling thoughts of fear and curiosity, when the angel said, "If you do not eat for 40 days I will give you this liquid."

The angel disappeared, but not my excitement or curiosity from the experience. My desire to taste the liquid was stronger than my fear of going without food.

I had no idea anyone could live without eating a day, much less 40. It seemed impossible, but the excitement and the desire never left me. Finally I made up my mind to do whatever it took to drink the liquid offered by the angel. It seemed impossible, but something inside me refused to give up.

One night, while attending a retreat in the Smoky Mountains of Tennessee, I spotted a strange colored light in the distance. My curiosity overcame any resistance to walk into the dark night to discover the source of the mystery.

After walking up and down the mountain for a couple of hours in the dark, I entered a cave with an eerie glow emanating from inside. I could hear music coming from deep below the entrance. My first thought was that people were camping and playing music inside.

However, the further I walked, the faster my heartbeat became and the more my emotions began to change. The light changed into colors I associated with melancholy until all at once I felt a sense of sadness. I began to weep uncontrollably and heard a voice inside me say, "Innocent blood is crying to be redeemed."

Immediately, turning around I saw a man sitting in a white robe on a rock and knew he was the source of the light and sound. I was unsure if I was dreaming or awake. His lips were not moving but I clearly understood his thoughts.

I was hypnotized by the beauty and serenity of this being and knew instantly it was the same man I had met as a young schoolboy.

His countenance had not changed, but this particular visit sent me to my knees weeping like a child. The compassion I felt at that moment was overwhelming. The man touched my shoulder, but it felt as if my insides were on fire. I immediately knew my life

Holy Spirit

22

was being used as an altar of sacrifice to atone for the injustice committed.

My weeping continued uncontrollably for hours until blood appeared on the surface of my skin. Suddenly, the light changed from amber to shades of violet. The sound reflected the change of the light in pitch and intensity.

My crying subsided and was replaced with a profound sense of joy and strength. The voice inside me said, "Intercession is a tool the Spirit uses to counteract evil and purify human vessels."

As I looked up I saw a cloud filled with men clothed in white worshiping the Lord. My tears of sadness turned to joy because I knew my intercession had been for each of them.

After leaving the cave it occurred to me that I had neither eaten nor drunk anything for several hours. The thought produced feelings of dehydration and hunger in me. My mind was racing wildly out of control with fear.

At once I heard a voice I recognized from the cave say, "Why are you frightened?" **That instant my heart seized control of my thoughts and I understood a peace that satisfied my hunger and thirst.**

The Holy Spirit was preparing me to understand the origin and construction of thoughts. It also became crystal clear to me why Jesus is the Prince of Peace.

The power resonating from that voice silenced all the voices of fear and panic created by my mind. I knew the time had come for me to taste the liquid offered to me years earlier.

CHAPTER 3

MY WAKE-UP CALL

Growing up, I lived around the beaches of Florida and learned to surf at an early age. The waves there were never really big compared with other places in the world.

After graduating from college, I moved to California and then lived in Hawaii to enjoy some of the larger waves. My fascination with waves was a distraction from the hunger in my soul for more of the supernatural.

I recall one day when I was surfing some large waves with a few friends. The current was strong, and we had become separated in the water during the course of the morning. The skies became ominous and the waves grew rougher. As I turned to paddle beyond the approaching set of waves something bumped my surfboard.

Every surfer hears the horror stories of shark attacks and is well aware of the ever-present danger in the oceans. Therefore, most beginners are more concerned about the creatures under the water than the waves breaking on top. The ones who become the best wave riders are the ones who are at peace in the ocean regardless of the animals below.

Nevertheless, my mind was actively creating images of danger and foreboding from the jarring of my surfboard. It was difficult to think of anything but the horror stories. As I was consumed in my fearful thoughts, a huge wave struck me unexpectedly.

The first rule of paddling a surfboard is to always be perpendicular to the wave. Well, I was not, and a huge wave separated me from my board, sending me to the bottom of the ocean.

Most surfers use a leash, which is a strong plastic tether connected to the board and attached by Velcro to one's ankle. This saves endless time swimming to shore to collect your board after wiping out on a wave. Furthermore, it offers some piece of mind to those a great distance from the shore.

This particular wave broke my leash and threw me like a rag doll to the ocean's floor. The immediate question, which floods one's head in that condition, concerns the issue of air and if your lungs have enough. The answer to that question is never known until it is tested in those terrifying conditions.

I tried desperately to find the bottom in order to push myself to the surface. Unfortunately, the pressure from the wave was equivalent to having several hundred pounds of weight strapped to my back. The effort I expended fighting against this force exhausted me and depleted the air in my lungs. My fear of drowning created panic, but the lack of oxygen prevented any physical resistance to what I imagined was certain death. As I resigned myself to the inevitable, something touched me that felt like a hot iron running down my spine and exiting through my navel.

Suddenly, tranquility beyond reason filled my head with thoughts and images reminiscent of my first angelic visitation. My spirit was engulfed with the love of my heavenly Father and transformed me into a dimension of "knowing" beyond anything I had ever experienced.

I had an overwhelming sense of peace about the situation and was no longer afraid to die. **It was as if the fear of drowning was my only attachment to the physical world.**

Loosing that attachment immediately opened the door to the feeling best described as love. The power of love swallowed up all of my fear.

Moreover, my mind experienced an event that appeared like watching a curtain fall. My thoughts were filled with joy, which had been hidden by the shroud of fear.

The love transformed my darkness to the most spectacular brilliant light I had ever seen. It penetrated and energized every cell and fiber of my being.

Instantly, I was filled with compassion for everyone I had harmed in thought or deed. **The eyes of my understanding were opened to the person of Jesus Christ and His amazing power of forgiveness. It was then I KNEW love, not in a concept but in a person.**

It was during those split seconds in time that I experienced unconditional love and forgiveness from Jesus. Immediately, my mind was filled with thanksgiving for all the things I had taken for granted that He had done. For example, I remembered when someone stopped me from an oncoming car in traffic, and the time the doorbell rang, waking me up just in time to put out a fire that had started in the kitchen. Memories of His mercy flooded my mind, and gratitude was flooding my soul. I learned later that this was the purest form of worship.

The next thing I remembered was sitting on the beach coughing and spitting out ocean water. I was never sure how I survived or why my surfboard lay beside me when I awoke. All I remember to this day was the amazing peace that flooded my soul. That encounter changed my life. The details of what happened must not be as important as the impact it left in my spirit and soul, otherwise I am confident the Holy Spirit would have shown me. One thing is certain my commitment to Christ and confidence in His destiny for my life has increased a hundredfold.

The Holy Spirit has reminded me many times that fear surrenders to love and those who know Christ will have encounters to test His power to deliver them from their worst horrors.

The spirit realm has become my refuge and strong tower. The Holy Spirit is my closest friend and ally; He knows my life is His to do as He pleases. Because of this, fasting has become a joy, not an effort, because I know the power of life is not in the physical dimension.

SECTION II

THE INVISIBLE WORLD

CHAPTER 4

PURPOSES AND BENEFITS OF FASTING

Fasting is one of the most powerful tools the Holy Spirit will use to manifest the mysteries of Christ and break preconceived ideas and doctrines. It is by no means the only method that facilitates our relationship with Christ but it is, in my opinion, the most powerful and profound way to meet Him face to face inside the spiritual dimension.

Most dictionaries define fasting as abstinence from food for varying lengths of time. Food is defined as nutrients or nourishment in solid form. Fasting in some cases has become an exotic term to imply sacrificing something you want or desire.

For example, there are some who stop watching TV or listening to music and refer to this as fasting. In my opinion, if one reduces the material stimuli from this world it can be beneficial. The benefit is increased tenfold if one fills that time with prayer.

People who watch the wrong types of movies over time will damage their emotional centers and desensitize their spirits.

I believe the Holy Spirit rewards those who will separate themselves from external stimuli to spend time with Him.

However, food is more than just a stimulus, because over time it will change our blood, which affects our organs, emotions, thoughts and future generations. Later in this book, you will see the connection between your blood and the Holy Spirit.

There are many ways to fast solid food, but fasting should not be confused with abstaining from water. Oxygen, water and sleep, in that order, are more important than food. Many people can live weeks without food but no one can survive more than a few minutes without oxygen.

The Bible describes various kinds of fasts and the different purposes associated with the sacrifice. Nehemiah, David, Anna, Jesus, Paul and Barnabas participated in **normal** fasts, abstaining from food for several weeks, but not water.

Daniel did not eat meat or sugar for twenty-one days as a **partial** fast. Esther is an example of an **extreme** fast because she did without food and drink for three days. Moses and Elijah are examples of **supernatural** fasting eating no bread or drinking no water for 40 days and nights.

Moses was there with the Lord forty days and forty nights; he ***ate no bread and drank no water.*** *And he wrote upon the tables the words of the covenant, the Ten Commandments.*

Exodus 34:28 AMP

Water is important to drink during a fast, and one should be clear about this in order to prevent the devil from destroying our temples. Those who are wise will listen carefully to the Holy Spirit and refrain from acting in the flesh or listening to the wrong voices.

One of the purposes of this book is to encourage all of those reading it to trust the Holy Spirit. You are alive today because He wants you to thrive and grow in the fullness and stature of Christ. Trust Him! For specific purposes and under the direction of the Holy Spirit I have undertaken extreme fasts on a number of occasions. The results were both physically and spiritually profound.

There are hundreds of books written about fasting, which describe methods and results. This book is less about ways to fast and more about the purposes for fasting. One of the primary reasons for writing this book is to provoke a divine hunger in those who want to experience the supernatural on a regular basis.

If one will take authority over physical appetites and make the smallest steps towards freedom from the slavery of food, one will recapture territory previously stolen and will be counted among those seizing God's Kingdom.

*But from the time of John the Baptist till now, the Kingdom of the Heaven has been suffering violent assault, **and the violent have been seizing it by force.***

Matthew 11:12 Weymouth

Everyone's initial struggles with fasting are the result of preconceived ideas and theologies. The violence spoken of by Jesus in Matthew should start with tearing down our strongholds and false images of Christ and His messages.

The cross is the battleground where our opinions, feelings, comforts and desires have no influence over our journey into His Kingdom. The most powerful secret weapon for that dismantling process is fasting.

In fact, the sooner one closes their mouth concerning food, and abandons excuses or opinions for past failures, the sooner one will experience freedom from those prisons. Fasting is the quickest and most powerful way to break open the doors holding you captive in your mind and body.

It is the most effective way of demonstrating to the powers and principalities your knowledge of Christ and His authority over them. Moreover, it displays the hope of His glory in your body and soul.

When I first read the above verse in Matthew, it sounded very contrary to my image of Jesus. My picture of Jesus was that of an innocent, sweet person carrying lambs on His shoulders, while healing the sick. That is the way religion has portrayed Him for centuries.

Jesus was violently opposed to the mentality of this world, particularly religion. He was so aggressive with the powers and principalities that they feared Him. **They were afraid**

because they knew He was prepared to give His life to destroy their authority.

Jesus understood that His death would be required to re-establish the kingdom stolen from Adam. Those who desire to be His disciples must be just as passionate. One cannot allow any obstacle or hindrance to prevent one from victory. Fasting is THE principal tool to display your determination to retake what you have surrendered through ignorance.

In my opinion, fasting is a lifestyle for every disciple. Fasting transformed my thoughts and has become my doorway into the spiritual realm.

The physical changes in your body will reflect the spiritual transition that has begun. Moreover, if you establish fasting as a lifestyle, the heavens will remain open in your life and mind. For those who fast, the atmosphere created by the Holy Spirit is impossible to describe with words.

This is the portal by which revelation enters our life and changes our consciousness. We will depend less and less on the material world for our resources and will experience the supernatural supply from the Holy Spirit as "our daily bread." This is the sustenance that supplies our physical bodies and nourishes our spirits.

Perhaps the most important impartation one could receive from this book is the absolute necessity to fast in order to change one's current condition. Also, if you are satisfied with your life and relationship with Christ, this book will only reinforce what you already know.

Many people reading this book may identify themselves as Christians according to accepted doctrines and scriptural interpretations. While this is an essential beginning, it is only the first step of a much deeper journey. Our initial images of Jesus as the Christ must continually ascend if our desire is to rule and reign with Him.

Every revelation of Christ we uncover unlocks treasures designed for our personal development and destiny.

CHAPTER 5

QUANTUM FASTING AND THE SUPERNATURAL

You may be asking what *fasting* and *quantum* have in relation with one another. From a natural point of view, they have nothing in common. Very little about fasting is natural. Fasting, as you will learn, is much more than just not eating.

My introduction to that word and its meaning was born from a desire to better communicate my experiences during and after fasting.

This chapter will explain the meaning and purpose behind the title of this book. Science interested me less in school than it does now, so my explanations will be from a layman's perspective. Scientists, like theologians, rarely agree with one another on information pertaining to data or the Bible, respectively, because most of their conclusions are formed from preconceived beliefs.

According to Webster's New Collegiate Dictionary, the definition of *science* is *knowledge attained through study or practice, or knowledge covering general truths of the operation of general laws, esp. as obtained and tested through scientific method [and] concerned with the physical world.*

As the definition indicates, science uses the information it gathers to form laws and theories about things still indefinable such as "reality," which according to the dictionary **is the state of things as they are or appear to be.**

However, the data is only as reliable as the instruments used to collect it. One of the fundamental purposes of research scientists is to discover principles that are reproducible outside the laboratory.

Nevertheless, it is impossible for human beings to be objective, because those designing the measuring devices have preconceived ideas of the results before the investigation is completed. Hence, the results will generally confirm the researcher's expectations. The opinions and theories concerning creation and the origin of man are formed from these methods.

Most intellectuals, particularly scientists, disregard the Bible and a personal God. They construct theories about life and man's origins from that position. In fact, most university professors assume that anyone who does not believe in evolution is ignorant.

I believe that anyone who forms their opinion about the origin of life from science needs more faith than those who believe the Bible. The inability of man to be objective is the door to pride and arrogance, which directly or indirectly impacts society.

According to Merriam Webster Dictionary *objective* means expressing or dealing with facts or conditions as perceived **without distortion by personal feelings, prejudices, or interpretations.**

The world is much more than man can measure with his instruments. Anyone who has had an encounter with Christ has experienced something undeniably real and immeasurable by man's instruments. However, the splitting of the atom began to change some of science's preconceived ideas.

They discovered a world their instruments were unable to measure but had undeniable influence over the material world. They stumbled upon a strange world that behaved differently from the physical dimension. This led to the formation of a branch of science called quantum physics, established to investigate discrete, indivisible units of energy called quanta.

Energy and matter are among the most important words in the vocabulary of physicists. Energy is the unknown power source behind all of the matter in the universe. Quantum theory is a form of theoretical physics with the sole purpose of understanding the fundamental properties of matter.

They discovered that energy and matter responded to influences beyond their reasoning or understanding. Moreover, their instruments could not accurately measure the results of most of their experiments.

The origin and relationship between the visible and invisible worlds remains a mystery for science, which has attempted to resolve it by studying energy and matter. Consequently, those investigations are uncovering more questions than answers.

We stated earlier that science uses the terms matter and energy to describe its research of the material world. Christians know that man is a spirit that temporarily resides in a material body. Science searches for answers about our origin from the invisible realm of energy because they refuse to acknowledge our spiritual identity.

*Let the LORD, **the God of the spirits of all flesh;** set a man over the congregation.*

Numbers 27:16 WEB

*Moreover, we had human parents to discipline us, and we respected them. Should we not be even more willing to be subject to the **Father of spirits** and live?*

Hebrews 12:9 NRSV

God is Spirit; and those who worship Him must bring Him true spiritual worship.

John 4:24 Weymouth

Science spends billions of dollars constructing instruments like a supercollider, which describes a machine that smashes subatomic particles together, hoping to discover the "god particle," or material that gives matter mass. In other words, physicists believe that the substance that formed the physical world after the big bang can be found by smashing sub-atomic matter particles together at the speed of light.

Therefore, their pursuits for answers concerning creation are from the material world instead of searching inside their own hearts. Nevertheless, they quickly learned that the invisible realm controls the visible world.

For what this world considers to be wisdom is nonsense in God's sight. As the scripture says, God traps the wise in their cleverness.

1 Corinthians 3:19 TEV

Faith is the tool and power Christians must use to understand the spiritual or invisible realm. Science generally will not believe what it cannot measure and, as a result, will never be able to understand the spiritual dimension.

Nevertheless, God is revealing Himself to the skeptics of this world including scientists. He is confounding the wise with the most fundamental properties of the material world called atoms. These are the building blocks for everything visible and invisible. The sun, air, water, planets, chairs, food and our bodies are all composed of atoms.

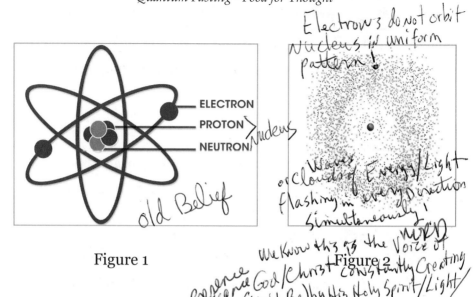

Handwritten annotations:

Electrons do not orbit Nucleus in uniform pattern!

or Clouds of Energy/Light Flashing in every direction Simultaneously!

We Know this as the Presence/Essence of God/Christ constantly creating (Light Be) by His Holy Spirit/Light/Energy/Power! the Voice of MXM!

ELECTRON
PROTON > Nucleus
NEUTRON

Old Belief

Figure 1   Figure 2

The scientists who established the traditional model of an atom held the belief that electrons orbited the nucleus of the atom much like planets rotate around the sun. However, the electron microscope discovered it was not that way at all. See Figure 1.

Their beliefs were inaccurate. Electrons do not orbit around the nucleus of an atom in a uniform pattern but are rather clouds of energy flashing in every direction simultaneously. See Figure 2.

This seems to indicate that electrons are in many places at the same time. The invisible world of energy is a mystery to science and does not conform to its theories and laws.

Atoms are 99.99% empty space. So, what prevents objects from passing through one another? Each atom vibrates at a certain frequency according to their composition of electrons, protons and neutrons. Electrons surrounding the atom form a cloud that either repels or attracts other atoms with the same vibration.

Therefore, it only appears as if you are walking on a concrete sidewalk. The electrons of the concrete are repelling the electrons on your sneakers and in reality you are hovering over the sidewalk. Research suggests these clouds or waves of electrons change or "blink" into view from time to time and form particles of matter. **This is important to understand because science is desperate to learn why energy becomes matter.**

It is also fascinating from a Christian's perspective to read the term blinking in the context of the letter Paul wrote to the Corinthians:

Quantum Leap

It will happen suddenly, quicker than the blink of an eye. At the sound of the last trumpet the dead will be raised. We will all be changed, so that we will never die again.

Our dead and decaying bodies will be changed into bodies that won't die or decay. (As in Resurrection Body of Christ)

I Corinthians 15: 51-52 CEV

(Light/Spirit)

The spiritual realm is what science calls energy. Christ determines what will be visible or invisible. Eternity resides inside of Christ, and Paul knew this after his encounter with Jesus on the Damascus road.

Christ

For in him were created all things in heaven and on earth, the visible and the invisible, whether thrones or dominions or principalities or powers; all things were created through him and for him. Christ — Christ

We Exist Because of Christ + for Christ/God Purposes/Plans!

Christ *outside of time + Always Existed (before Time was Created)*

He is (before all things,) and in him all things hold together *(He Alone, By His Word causes All Life to Be!) Christ*

✗ *Colossians 1:16-17 NAB*

✗ Paul's encounter on the road to Damascus was profound, and it was necessary for him to fast from food and drink for three days to receive spiritual revelation that the church today still does not fully understand. *Fasting does not give You Favor with God, We already have Favor because of Jesus Finishing All things on the Cross + Resurrection (Paul)*

And for three days he was not able to see, and he took no food or drink. *Fasting puts us Above the Flesh/Physical Existence (which is Always controlling our Spirit)... So we need to Ask Holy Spirit how He wants us to Fast (Safely), So we can (our spirit) suppress the flesh + soul to allow Spirit to be in Control! (will, Emotions, Thoughts)*

Acts 9:9 BBE
TO SEE / BE

But the Lord said to him, Go, for this man is a chosen instrument of Mine to bear My name before the Gentiles and kings and the descendants of Israel; *Enlightened by Holy Spirit (taught His Truth, Wisdom, Ways, etc) So that we can Live By the Spirit to Spirit, Set Free from Flesh/Earth Womb + Worship +*

For I will make clear to him how much he will be afflicted and must endure and suffer for My name's sake. *Live in Spirit (Christ) + Truth to do His Will (Father) on Earth as it is in Heaven!*

Acts 9:15-16 AMP

✗ The authority over the visible world begins with a relationship with the author of both dimensions. The voice of Christ is the *Light Be* invisible and immeasurable frequency uniting all things in the material world. The sound of His Word creates energy and forms matter. Those who have had a personal encounter with Christ know His voice. The sound of His voice is the frequency of life, both visible and invisible. The invisible world of energy materializes into the physical through a phenomenon known as a "collapsed wave function." This describes the process of electrons materializing from the invisible dimension of energy into the physical world of matter. The reasons for this have been the topic of research for years.

Electrical fields of unseen energy surround all organic life. The energy from human beings emits frequencies or vibrations consistent with the individual. Science has determined that energy becomes matter after the cloud or energy surrounding the atom encounters a frequency or vibration that alters its electromagnetic field. *Both Positive or Negative thinking is Energy & will attract what we focus thoughts upon! His Word says* **The energy from the person observing the invisible world directly affects the nature and character of the atom, changing it from energy to matter.** *Seek 1st Him (Set focus/Heart & Mind on Christ to Draw His Spirit into our Physical Realm & to Draw Our Being into His Spirit (outside of Time), His Kingdom,* The unseen world is directly affected by our spiritual nature in ways that create divine meetings with the Holy Spirit. These *His* clandestine rendezvous are designed for us to meet our heavenly Father. *Righteousness & then All thing will be added to us (Here & Now) Set your Heart (Passion) on Him things Above* Consciousness is another way of describing the energy a person *where* releases because of his or her beliefs. Therefore, when one prays *you* or thinks about something invisible, that energy interacts with *are* the electromagnetic shell around those invisible atoms, which *Seated* changes energy into matter. *in Christ (as Spirit because we Believe & are Saved) Faith*

Now faith is the reality [TRUTH] of what is hoped for, the proof of what is not seen.

Hebrews 11:1 HCBS

In other words, the unseen world is filled with limitless potentials "waiting" for activation from someone. Therefore, according to science, the act of observation is both the cause and effect in the creation of the material universe. Furthermore, the observer subconsciously determines the reality of his world through preconceived beliefs.

In essence, there can be no objective study of the invisible world because individuals unintentionally interfere with their "reality." Each person finds the results they predict and are generally unaware of their subconscious participation in the outcome.

Hence, our physical world is not solid, but rather energy [Light/Spirit] and matter whirling at lightening speeds, producing the illusion of solidity. The reality of that illusion is further compounded by the collective consciousness of society.

For example, education and the media are responsible for perpetuating the belief that without a flu vaccination a widespread flu epidemic would result. This forms a consciousness or belief among people that medicine and physicians are the answer to sickness and disease.

There is very little man can do to change the collective consciousness, which has produced our current material world.

In other words, we have inherited the present day "collapsed wave functions."

But our personal life can be changed through the principles of Christ and His Kingdom, and even science is verifying the words of our Lord.

And Jesus said, [You say to Me], If You can do anything? [Why,] all things can be (are possible) to him who believes!

Mark 9:23 AMP

It has been my experience to see the invisible realm on a number of occasions beginning with the angelic visitations I described earlier. The Holy Spirit also opened my spiritual eyes to witness and understand the power separating the two realms as well as the darkness covering the minds of people.

Then Elisha prayed, "LORD, please open his eyes and let him see." So the LORD opened the servant's eyes. He looked and saw that the mountain was covered with horses and chariots of fire all around Elisha.

2 Kings 6:17 HCBS

Moreover, He explained that the Kingdom of God was only visible to those whose spirit was transformed through a rebirth into His Spirit, because the invisible realm vibrates at frequencies too high for the natural eyes to see.

Jesus answered him, I assure you, most solemnly I tell you, that unless a person is born again (anew, from above), he cannot ever see (know, be acquainted with, and experience) the kingdom of God.

John 3:3 AMP

Science has documented man's effect on matter through the interaction of his electromagnetic field. The analogy of a satellite transmitting signals or energy, which we receive on television, is an example of the way human beings are constructed.

Moreover, we are designed to both send and receive signals. Most people would assume our mind to be the source of the body's transmission.

However, the latest research indicates that our heart, or spirit as the Bible calls it, produces the strongest frequencies, which can alter the physical field of atoms surrounding us.

In other words, science believes the invisible energy emitted from the heart of man is stronger than his mental activity. Again the Bible, written before today's instruments, is at the forefront of modern technological discoveries.

For as he thinks in his heart, so is he.

Proverbs 23:7 NKJV

*For where **your treasure is, there will your heart** be also.*

Matthew 6:21 AMP

*Out of **your heart** come evil thoughts, murder, unfaithfulness in marriage, vulgar deeds, stealing, telling lies, and insulting others.*

Out of your Heart the Mouth Speaks!

Matthew 15:19 CEV

*I tell you the truth, if someone says to this mountain, 'Be lifted up and thrown into the sea,' and does not doubt in his **heart but believes** that what he says will happen, it will be done for him.*

Mark 11:23 NET

Science confirms what those whose spirits are immersed into Christ are experiencing. The heart of man was designed to be God's tabernacle and to have dominion over his soul (thinking) and body. In fact, the mind of man will never be converted until this transformation occurs, because their thoughts will be at the frequency of the material world, not God's Kingdom.

The spirit of man is the source of faith, but faith without love will not change circumstances in the natural world. The heart is the source of love because it originated from the heart of God. Love is heaven's frequency because it is the DNA of the creator and the substance of all things.

51

And now abide faith, hope, love, these three; but the greatest of these is love.

1 Corinthians 13:13 NKJV

He who does not love does not know God, for **God is love.**

1 John 4:8 NKJV

And we have known and believed the love that God has for us. ***God is love, and he who abides in love abides in God, and God in him.***

1 John 4:16 NKJV

Love is the frequency of God, and faith is the antenna necessary to see and hear Him. The reason man doesn't believe is because his mind is the receiver, not his heart.

The importance of this discovery should redefine your faith. If Christians would do whatever it takes to understand their spiritual nature, their world and future generations would never be the same.

Christians whose spirits are connected to God will witness the material of heaven manifesting on earth, or what science calls a "collapsed wave function." Fasting changed my frequency and extended my antenna.

Quantum fasting describes my experiences beyond the sacrifice of food. I use the term quantum as way to bridge the visible and invisible realms. It is more about the results of fasting than a method.

Those who hunger for His presence and make fasting a lifestyle will experience places inside Him reserved for disciples or disciplined ones. There one will discover the treasures too wonderful for words and more valuable than physical life itself.

Therefore, for me **quantum fasting is the visible sacrifice of food in order to partake of the divine nature of God.**

As His divine power has given to us all things that pertain to life and godliness, through the knowledge of Him who called us by glory and virtue, by which have been given to us exceedingly great and precious promises, that through these **you may be partakers of the divine nature,** *having escaped the corruption that is in the world through lust.*

2 Peter 1:3-4 NKJV

Fasting is for my spirit what oxygen is for my body. Fasting reduces the material stimuli for the physical body, thereby increasing the awareness of the invisible world of quanta.

This type of fasting represents a physical step into an invisible portal that can lead to experiences with Christ. It is the quickest way to effectively divorce oneself from the material world.

I truly believe that living without food for extended periods of time allowed the Holy Spirit to restructure my mind.

Fasting changed my life from the inside out and exposed me to the reality of Christ. Every experience has become a perpetual fountain bubbling up with fresh revelation each day. Today's revelation of Jesus is just enough to make me thirsty for tomorrow.

The world we experience in our physical body is validated through our five sense organs. They are composed of the nose, hands, ears, tongue and eyes. However, each of us has a spirit and soul constructed from materials not discernable by our senses.

Fasting feeds my spirit and starves my senses, creating an atmosphere of silence inside my body and mind. The longer I fast the greater His presence becomes, ushering in more of His peace and tranquility.

Fasting creates a knowing inside your being, which transcends emotions or feelings from the natural world. Your mind is awakened to the reality of Christ. His words are an ever-expanding dimension of eternity that requires spiritual understanding.

Perhaps one of the greatest benefits of quantum fasting for me was the ability to remain at peace after discovering my beliefs were formed primarily from my five senses. This discovery opened my eyes to the reality of Christ and His Kingdom in my midst.

Fasting made it painfully clear that my experiences with God and His Word were very shallow because I had no personal revelation of Him. It was only after fasting that my individual encounters increased to the point where He could teach me His ways.

John identified Jesus as the Word of God, the One who is the source of both the invisible and visible worlds. His Word is the invisible atomic structure holding everything together. I capitalize the W in word to illustrate that He, Jesus, is who and what He says He is.

In the beginning was the Word, and the Word was with God, and the Word was God.

And the Word became flesh and dwelt among us, and we beheld His glory, the glory as of the only begotten of the Father, full of grace and truth.

John 1: 1,14 NKJV

And He Himself existed before all things, and in Him all things consist (cohere, are held together).

Colossians 1:17 AMP

The Word was the source of life, and this life brought light to people.

John 1:4 TEV

Jesus said the world loves darkness more than the light. **Therefore, when man constructs his life and beliefs from a mind void of Christ the result will be more darkness.**

*And **the light** shines in the darkness, and the darkness did not comprehend it.*

John 1:5 NKJV

And this is the judgment, that the light has come into the world, and people loved darkness rather than light because their deeds were evil.

John 3:19 NRSV

Once more Jesus addressed them. I am the Light of the world, He said; the man who follows me shall certainly not walk in the dark, but shall have the light of Life.

John 8:12 Weymouth

The study of light and its properties has unlocked many treasures hidden in the universe. The result has made our life on earth much more convenient as it relates to travel, communication and creature comforts. It is perhaps one of the most studied phenomena in science because of its direct correlation with life. Indeed, that is a correct assumption for anyone who has reads the Bible.

Then God said, Let there be light; and there was light.

Genesis 1:3 NKJV

Everything came into existence through him. Not one thing that exists was made without him.

He was the source of life, and that life was the light for humanity.

John 1:3-4 GW

However, the light spoken of in the above scripture is not the same as that being studied by science. I believe the above scripture represents God releasing His glory, or eternal intelligence, into the universe, which is the light and life of mankind. The light of the sun, moon and stars was not created until the fourth day in the book of Genesis.

God made the two great lights—the greater light to rule the day and the lesser light to rule the night—and the stars.

God set them in the dome of the sky to give light upon the earth, to rule over the day and over the night, and to separate the light from the darkness. And God saw that it was good.

And there was evening and there was morning, the fourth day.

Genesis 1:16-19 NRSV

The light studied by science is the by-product of the original light and is formed by shadows and time. Although it is necessary for physical life in the material world, it is not The Light, which has no shadows and originates from within God.

Every good present and every perfect gift comes from above, from the Father who made the sun, moon, and stars. The Father doesn't change like the shifting shadows produced by the sun and the moon.

James 1:17 GW

Man makes his choices and discoveries of the universe from the shadows and illusions of the light outside of God. Without experiencing the glory of God in Christ, our minds are incapable of discerning the true light.

For with you is the fountain of life: **in your light we will see light.**

Psalm 36:9 BBE

Our marvelous universe was created for man to discover God as the author of life in the material and invisible worlds. Indeed, those who have been "born into" Christ are experiencing eternity and that reality now.

If you are experiencing sin, sickness and disease, it is because you are forming an image of Christ from the wrong light. Those whose spirits have been awakened in Christ reside in His Light, which illuminates both visible and invisible worlds.

And His appearance underwent a change in their presence; and His face shone clear and bright like the sun, and His clothing became as white as light.

Matthew 17:2 AMP

The scripture above is not just a story to fill pages in the Bible. The authority over darkness and hell is found in a true experience with Christ, which will make darkness flee. It will not happen through methods and doctrines, but an actual face-to-face encounter. That experience is a guarantee for those who will dedicate their lives to fasting and prayer.

Fasting is a powerful tool, which changes the chemistry of the body and allows the glory of God to penetrate our hearts and minds to reveal the true Light.

The light of Christ is the source and energy of all life. His words alone are the atoms that sustain the material world, and His words created the multi-dimensional heavens for His sons to enjoy.

Jesus re-established the Kingdom of God on earth to demonstrate His authority and power over all the forces of the fourth day's light. His miracles and resurrection were proof of

His domination over sin, sickness and death. Christians should not regard physical or medical science as the final word on man's origin or his health and healing. Their findings and diagnosis in most cases are the result of conclusions constructed from minds that have no regard for God.

Over the centuries science has discovered some of the laws God used to create and maintain our majestic universe, but they will never find the source or origins until they submit to Christ as Lord. The same is true for those who profess to be Christians but trust in the words of men more than those of Jesus.

Our creator designed us to live in the physical world but to access Him with our spirit. Otherwise, our lives will be one of conflict between the soul and body. Without spiritual understanding, the soul and body are helpless in discerning the right choices in a world ruled by their senses. Unfortunately, most of the world lives in this chaos, oblivious to the reality of the invisible realm.

Some people will experience feelings and sensations outside the limits of their senses. Those events create a hunger to know the origin and creator of these things. "Something" deep inside all human beings knows there is more than what our senses detect. That "something" is the sleeping spirit of man crying to be heard.

Do not surrender to the emotions or sensations you have believed to be real. There is nothing to fear, if you have truly passed from death to life through your trust in Christ.

Darkness and evil know that once you begin to fast, their hold over you is in jeopardy. The choice is yours. It has always been yours unless you relinquish it to the fear and doubt that your victory was guaranteed at the cross.

Quantum fasting describes the experience of all who have determined to nail their preconceived ideas and doctrines of Christ to His cross, beginning with food.

Those who expose themselves to this lifestyle will discover the manifold wisdom of Christ and the power to operate in the spirit realm. This requires dethroning the mind from its position of authority and power. In order to change the way we think, we must have our spirit awakened and fully activated by the Holy Spirit.

The baptism of the Holy Spirit is perhaps one of the most misunderstood power tools released on earth through Jesus. After an immersion in the Holy Spirit, one will be less concerned about whether speaking in tongues is of God. The first priority will be to "feed" your spirit, not your flesh.

One of the evidences of those baptized in the Holy Spirit is how little they open their mouths for food and idle conversation. Many times the Holy Spirit will speak to me during mealtime, and on many occasions I have excused myself and gone to listen.

One of the most profound things I learned through fasting is that Adam fell by opening his mouth to eat. Therefore, the longer my mouth is closed, the greater the opportunity to be fed by the Holy Spirit. Jesus told His disciples that His hment did not depend on the natural world.

Jesus told them, I have food to eat that you don't know about.

John 4:32 GW

Quantum physics has demonstrated it has no solutions to the questions of man's origin or purpose. The more they search to understand the mysteries of God without recognizing His supremacy, the more questions they uncover.

Nevertheless, the study of the subatomic world has provided a language for us who have been transformed by Christ to communicate with unbelievers. The world at large depends on science to solve their problems and satisfy the void inside their soul, which is an unconscious longing to know Christ.

Physicists have concluded our world to be an endless sea of energy with an infinite amount of possibilities. Therefore, our minds convert energy into matter through experiences, beliefs and traditions. Moreover, they believe the universe and our world are illusions created from the perceptions of the mind. Furthermore, if our minds did not shape and configure our world, the universe would simply remain an endless sea of atoms with countless possibilities.

If you exchange the words energy for spirit and matter for material it is easier to translate the results of science into Biblical terms. The following verses answer all the problems of science, but unbelief creates more questions than answers.

For everything, absolutely everything, above and below, visible and invisible, rank after rank after rank of angels—everything got started in him and finds its purpose in him.

He was there before any of it came into existence and holds it all together right up to this moment.

Colossians 1:16-17 Message

The source of that energy, which forms the relationships among all material objects, is Christ. More importantly, without His consent their ability to breathe or ask questions would cease to exist. Jesus is the source connecting our atoms to Him in the material world. His Word is the vibrational frequency holding all matter together, and if that tone changes, our atomic structures would dissolve.

Quantum fasting allows us access to our spirit, soul and body, while uncovering hidden events that took place before the foundation of the world. God is the creator of all spirits and the source of all creation, which means that our DNA is founded inside the One who formed us in His image and likeness.

Christ

Jesus is all in all, which means inside and outside of time He remains the constant before, during and after all conscious experiences of life. Beyond time God is. Eternity lives inside God because in Him there is no start or finish. Eternity does not begin when we die as so many believe. Christ is eternity and those who taste Him never die. *(a) Consciousness*

ONE Spirit in the Lord

The bread, which comes from heaven, is such bread that a man may take it for food and never see death.

John 6:50 BBE

The spiritual realm is multidimensional, which is why the church is so helpless to explain the scriptures. The ability to understand the Bible requires a spiritual knowledge not found in the material world.

The following sections will explain the power of quantum fasting on our triune beings. Each distinct nature of our being is intricately entwined with each other and requires spiritual surgery conducted by the Holy Spirit through fasting.

Nothing is more rewarding than to be taken apart, cleaned up and put back together by the One who created us. The quicker we submit to His way, the sooner we obtain access to the presence of an angelic host ministering to our every need.

SECTION III

SPIRIT

And the God of the peace Himself sanctify you wholly, and may your whole spirit, and soul, and body, be preserved blameless in the presence of our Lord Jesus Christ;

1 Thessalonians 5:23 YNG

God separated man into a three—part being to rule with Him in both the physical and spiritual dimensions. The power of fasting transcends both realms and will effectively purify each nature of man—body, soul and spirit. This book will familiarize the reader with the power of fasting in each nature.

The spirit of man is the most important part, because it is the one whose nature and characteristics most resemble the Father. Those who fast for extended periods of time have access to areas inside God few people experience.

These places are filled with treasures this world could not appreciate. Jesus told the Pharisees in Luke 16:15, *"The things of this world considered valuable by men are an abomination to God."* The power of the thoughts of the Holy Spirit in the spiritual realm has created an earthquake inside my spirit, which to this day continues to awaken greater revelations of Christ and **His finished work.**

CHAPTER 6

MY WORDS ARE SPIRIT AND LIFE

One of the most important statements in all the scriptures was made by Jesus and is found in John 6:63. I have included several translations to emphasize the importance of this scripture.

*It is the spirit that gives life; **the flesh is useless.** The words that I have spoken to you are spirit and life.*

NRSV

Life is spiritual. *Your physical existence doesn't contribute to that life. The words that I have spoken to you are spiritual. They are life.*

God's Word

It is the spirit, which gives Life. **The flesh confers no benefit whatever.** *The words I have spoken to you are **spirit and are Life.***

Weymouth

*The Spirit is the life giver; **the flesh is of no value:** the words, which, I have said to you, are **spirit and they are life.***

BBE

Perhaps the translation in the God's Word version illustrates why mankind is at such a disadvantage. The physical world is difficult enough to understand, but if one adds the pressures of family, job and money there is little time remaining to contemplate an invisible world.

Jesus says the flesh has no value, yet I discovered Him that way, which means my definition of flesh must be different from His. In fact the dictionary calls flesh the soft substance of a human or other animal body, consisting of muscle and fatty tissue.

That means the figure we see in the mirror is not the person Jesus died to save. Furthermore, it should not be the one who makes choices and decisions according to feelings or emotions.

Therefore, Jesus is in essence explaining to the Jews that their physical laws such as washing their hands and cups are of no value to God.

Nonetheless, God gave them those laws in hopes they would search for the spiritual connection of holiness. Your spirit is who you are, and it lives from the life inside the words He speaks. If He stops speaking to you or me, we will cease to exist.

The Master however said to him, "Here we see how you Pharisees

*clean the outside of the cup or plate, while your secret hearts are
full of greed and selfishness.*

Luke 11:39 Weymouth

*"Woe to you, scribes and Pharisees, hypocrites! For you clean
the outside of the cup and of the plate, but inside they are full of
greed and self-indulgence.*

Matt. 23:25 NRSV

One of the most important keys for both entering and
understanding the spiritual world is fasting. Also, the battle to
return to our spiritual nature is the journey that must begin with
fasting. Jesus illustrated this after He was baptized.

Jesus came from the invisible realm to speak words of the
Spirit that require spiritual understanding. If we are to
comprehend the Bible or the words He spoke we must hear
and see spiritually.

His words are the only containers of life, because He is the life of
every creature. **The quantum world of physics recognizes a
connection between all material substances and energy.**
If we exchange the word energy for spirit a parallel can be drawn
between the Bible and science.

*Everything came into existence through him. Not one thing that
exists was made without him.*

He was the source of life, and that life was the light for humanity.

John 1:3-4 GW

For it was in Him that all things were created, in heaven and on earth, things seen and things unseen, whether thrones, dominions, rulers, or authorities; all things were created and exist through Him and in and for Him.

And He Himself existed before all things, and in Him all things consist.

Colossians 1:16-17 AMP

CHAPTER 7

OUR SPIRIT IS HIS KEY

In order to truly understand the nature of our spirit and its authority over the physical world, it is necessary to fast from food. *[handwritten: Key to Christ Realm,]*

Most Christians agree that man is a spirit with a soul and body. The challenge begins when we attempt to understand the makeup and purposes of each of these three natures. Fasting is the only tool I have discovered that unveils each distinct person and purpose hidden inside each nature.

....and the God of the peace Himself sanctify you wholly, and may your whole **spirit, and soul, and body,** *be preserved blameless in the presence of our Lord Jesus Christ;*

1 Thessalonians 5:23 YNG

The physical Son of God, Jesus, was described in the verse below to contain the Father and Spirit. Jesus represented the perfect model of spirit, soul and body sanctified wholly.

For in him all the fullness of the Godhead dwells bodily,

Colossians 2:9 WEB

The Father, Son and Holy Spirit are one and separate simultaneously, which is why God formed man "*in His image and likeness*" (Genesis 1:26).

God is Spirit, and those who worship Him must worship in spirit and truth.

John 4:24 NKJV

This is the nature of God, which provides man with his true identity and purpose. After man's disobedience, his spiritual nature was no longer in control, creating an imbalance in his thinking and character. From this position man attempts to uncover his origin and purpose. This is tantamount to rowing a boat with one paddle. The trip will consist of meaningless circles no closer to his destination than when the journey began.

The spiritual void inside mankind is responsible for the tribulations of this world. This is critical to understand if one is honest about discovering the truth of his place and purpose on earth. Otherwise, one will be overwhelmed by the fear and unbelief rampant among those whose spirits are not connected to God.

If man needed nothing more than his body and brain to discover his origin, the world would be free of sin, sickness, disease and death. Man is unable to discover the answers that could change the world. The first step begins with acknowledging that Christ is who He said He was. In addition, the church that should be leading the change has, in many cases, neglected to train people about their spiritual natures.

*Thus says the LORD, who spreads out the heavens, lays the foundations of the earth, and **forms the spirit of man within him:***

Zechariah 12:1 NAB

Man is helpless until he finds his true Father, but until he discovers that truth for himself he will not bow before Jesus. Neither religion nor politics will provide his spiritual DNA or mediate that encounter.

One must search for the truth outside the boundaries of preconceived ideas and theology. Fasting brought me face to face with the Person who is the truth and the life and the only way back to my spiritual inheritance.

Fasting is the only method of preparation for this type of spiritual encounter. Jesus had fasted 40 days before the devil approached Him. The temptations most of us encounter are not face to face with satan. (I refuse to capitalize satan because it would attribute honor to one Jesus calls a liar, thief and murder) He does not waste time with those who are not capable of controlling their most basic desires such as eating.

The only way to ~~threaten~~ the ~~devil~~ and get the attention of heaven is to quit feeding your body and mind with the material from this dimension.

[handwritten: Step out of Human (Consciousness)]

The greatest majority of people in the churches are easy targets for demonic influence because of either overeating or consuming the wrong foods. Demons require a physical host void of spiritual power. **Feed your spirit and starve your body to achieve victory over those forces!**

If you stop eating and begin praying for someone other than yourself, hell and heaven will take notice. They will not necessarily see you from the same dimension, but they will recognize the frequency or vibration resonating from you.

Then Noah built an altar to the LORD, and choosing from every clean animal and every clean bird, he offered holocausts on the altar.

When the LORD smelled the sweet odor, he said to himself: "Never again will I doom the earth because of man, since the desires of man's heart are evil from the start; nor will I ever again strike down all living beings, as I have done.

Genesis 8:20-21 NAB

God made a covenant with Noah never to destroy this planet or man again and demonstrated it with a rainbow. The covenant was the foreshadow God would make through His Son. That covenant offers redemption to man and spiritual authority in the physical world.

If God smells a sweet aroma from our flesh 'burning' on the altar of fasting, He will send the Holy Spirit. Quantum fasting is the tool that exposes our soul and spirit to the mind of Christ. That condition creates a scent and a different frequency in our bodies.

Remember, quantum fasting is the experience one will achieve beyond the sacrifice of food and becomes the vehicle for understanding the spiritual nature of God. track DNA and

CHAPTER 8

JESUS THE LIVING WORD

I knew that Jesus fasted before He began preaching His kingdom, and that provoked me to read what He said. If His words are spirit, I needed to activate my spirit to understand Him. I determined that fasting would be the tool necessary for this activation.

The scriptures describe men and women whose fasting, along with prayers, altered events and circumstances during their lives. Those who sacrificed food for the presence of God changed their world, and I was determined to do the same. Furthermore, after fasting, my experiences with angels became more the norm for me than most Christians.

Jesus demonstrated His mastery over the material world with miracles. He returned from the wilderness after fasting 40 days, which I believe prepared His mind and body for His death and resurrection.

In my opinion, fasting was a crucial building block in

constructing His resurrection consciousness over death.

*Then Jesus went back **full of and under the power of the [Holy] Spirit** into Galilee, and the fame of Him spread through the whole region round about.*

Luke 4:14 AMP

Jesus drank water while fasting, which is why the Bible says, *"Afterward He was hungry"* (Luke 4:2). *According to the scriptures*, the devil tempted Jesus by suggesting He change stones to bread. However, he soon discovered that Jesus preferred "manna," or the word of God, rather than physical food.

Jesus answered him, saying, It is written, Man shall not live by bread alone, but by every word of God.

Luke 4:4 WEB

Jesus is the living Word, and He also represented the manna in the wilderness during the time of Moses. The amazing revelations inside the scriptures remain hidden to those who do not "eat and drink" from Him.

I am the living bread, which has come from heaven: *if any man takes this bread for food he will have life forever: and more than this, the bread, which I will give, is my flesh which I will give for the life of the world.*

*Then the Jews had an angry discussion among themselves, saying, How is it possible for this man to give us his **flesh for food?***

*Then Jesus said to them, truly I say to you, If you do not take the flesh of the Son of man for food, and if you do not take his blood for drink, **you have no life in you.***

He who takes my flesh for food and my blood for drink has eternal life: and I will take him up from the dead at the last day.

John 6:51-54 BBE

Pay close attention to the words of Jesus in verse 53, *"you have no life in you."* In other words, "life" must be something more than a heartbeat and breathing.

Therefore, feeding on the body and blood of Jesus is the only nourishment capable of producing "real life." That sounds preposterous until you understand the reality of the spiritual world, whose author and master is Christ.

Religion, society, education and the "world system" in general are anti-Christ because the father of that consciousness is satan. The mindset of the visible world is constructed from pride and selfishness.

The present physical world is a reflection of satan's nature and has been reproduced throughout the history of mankind, beginning with Adam's fall.

It is a mindset or consciousness that perpetuates fear and greed. **Quantum fasting is the vehicle to go beyond our physical senses and explore the nature and mind of Christ from within the spiritual realm.**

My theology changed about "needing" Jesus to return in a physical body once I understood my spiritual nature. My encounters with Christ in the spiritual realm gave me the understanding of the dominion of the invisible world over the physical. **Nevertheless, most of us have been taught to expect a physical manifestation to solve a spiritual problem.**

Then Jesus said to them, truly I say to you, If you do not take the flesh of the Son of man for food, and if you do not take his blood for drink, you have no life in you.

*He who takes my flesh for food and my blood for drink has eternal life: and I will take him up from the dead at the **last day**.*

John 6:53-54 BBE

The "last day" mentioned in verse 54 refers to a specific period in one's life after discovering the "life" Jesus speaks of in verse 53. Otherwise, those who walk the earth are physically alive but spiritually dead and, according to Jesus, "have no life."

Our minds in their current condition are incapable of understanding that because of years of wrong teaching mixed with fear. **Until each of us encounters the new birth into Christ, we will be unable to comprehend the spiritual Word as Christ.** The following scriptures are not just words on paper but a mirror for self-examination.

Jesus said to her, I am the one who brings people back to life, and I am life itself. Those who believe in me will live even if they die.

John 11:25 GW

If you love your life, you will lose it. If you give it up in this world, you will be given eternal life.

John 12:25 CEV

Each of the verses above demonstrates a power emanating from the Spirit of one who has already conquered death and stands eternally ready to change your future.

One of the biggest problems preventing the church from understanding the words of Christ is their preoccupation with eating physical food instead of feasting on the body and blood of Christ.

Quantum fasting will train a believer to resist physical gratification in order to obtain spiritual revelation.

If we sacrifice physical food for His presence, He will nourish us with manna. We recall the Israelites were fed the "living Word" even before He came in the flesh.

Remember that for 40 years the Lord your God led you on your journey in the desert. He did this in order to humble you and test you. He wanted to know whether or not you would wholeheartedly obey his commands.

So he made you suffer from hunger and then fed you with manna, which neither you nor your ancestors had seen before. He did this to teach you that a person cannot live on bread alone but on every word that the Lord speaks.

Deuteronomy 8:2-3 GW

Jesus used the word of the Law to defeat the devil in the wilderness. Jesus passed the test in the wilderness after 40 days. The Israelites died in the wilderness after 40 years eating the Word, in the form of manna but never allowed the Word to change them.

Examine this scripture and allow it to impact you as it did me.

For indeed the gospel was preached to us as well as to them; but the word, which they heard did not profit them, not being mixed with faith in those who heard it.

Hebrews 4:2 NKJV

The "gospel" was preached to the Old Testament Jews in the times of Moses. The gospel is Christ, and whether He is manna or Jesus, God's message is the same. **Quit feeding on the material world and eat the "living word" in order to live free from sin, sickness and death.**

The gospel messages most people hear today are void of power because they are constructed from the material world. The true message of the gospel is spiritual through and through because it consists of the "living Word." Jesus was the manifestation of the spiritual world and carried His Father's DNA. **The power over the physical world is hidden in the invisible.**

CHAPTER 9

STONES TO BREAD

*So the Tempter came and said, (If you are the Son of God,)
command these stones to turn into loaves.*

Matthew 4:3 Weymouth

[handwritten annotations: Identity: We are Beloved Sons/Daughters of God; Co-Heirs of Kingdom with Christ. A Royal Priesthood. Devil was Defeated + Authority given back to us over the Earth! (Are you Really Son of God?)]

The question from the devil in the above scripture reveals the
nature of the serpent. His goal was to corrupt the mind of Jesus
and pollute His blood, which would prevent Him from fulfilling
His purpose as our redeemer.

Therefore, his suggestion for Jesus to turn stones into bread was
the same as saying (author paraphrasing) break your covenant
with your Father and serve me.

Jesus answered each temptation of the devil with the written
Word, and as The Word, which existed before the Garden of Eden.
The Word was, is and will be the final authority over all evil.
[handwritten: (Jesus)]

I am the Alpha and the Omega, the Beginning and the End, says the Lord God, He Who is and Who was and Who is to come, the Almighty (the Ruler of all).

Revelation 1:8 AMP

The devil also wants to pervert and corrupt the mind of man with thoughts of doubt about his relationship with his heavenly Father, as he did with the woman in the Garden. He appeals to our senses today the same way he did then.

Stones are used throughout the scriptures to represent covenant. The first house of God was dedicated on the stone Jacob used for a pillow. God gave the Law to Moses on stone tablets.

Then Jacob rose early in the morning, and took the stone that he had put at his head, set it up as a pillar, and poured oil on top of it.

And this stone, which I have set as a pillar shall be God's house, and of all that You give me I will surely give a tenth to You.

Genesis 28:18,22 NKJ

When I went up the mountain to receive the tables of stone, the tables of the covenant which the Lord made with you, I remained on the mountain forty days and forty nights; I neither ate food nor drank water.

Deuteronomy 9:9 AMP

Our lives are more than food or drink, but if we do not fast and pray the devil will lead us around by our stomach. An example of how food caused a man to break covenant with God is the story of Jacob and Esau. The original plan of God was to pass the largest inheritance, both spiritual and physical, to a father's firstborn son. But the eldest son of Isaac, Esau, sold his covenant birthright for food.

And Esau said to Jacob, I beg of you, let me have some of that red lentil stew to eat, for I am faint and famished! That is why his name was called Edom [red].

Jacob answered, Then sell me today your birthright (the rights of a firstborn).

(Sell Soul to devil)

Esau said, See here, I am at the point of death; what good can this birthright do me?

Jacob said, Swear to me today [that you are selling it to me]; and he swore to [Jacob] and sold him his birthright.

Then Jacob gave Esau bread and stew of lentils, and he ate and drank and rose up and went his way. Thus Esau scorned his birthright as beneath his notice.

Genesis 25:30-34 AMP

Even as it is written, Jacob I loved, but Esau I hated.

Romans 9:13 WEB

The devil is lawless. Those who break covenant, as he did, are lawless and consequently lose their birthright. **Sin has corrupted mans bloodline.** Paul says it clearly in Romans 3.

Since all have sinned and are falling short of the honor and glory which God bestows and receives.

All are justified and made upright and in right standing with God, freely and gratuitously by His grace (His unmerited favor and mercy), through the redemption which is [provided] in Christ Jesus,

Whom, God put forward, before the eyes of all, as a mercy seat and propitiation by His blood, through faith. This was to show God's righteousness, because in His divine forbearance He had passed over and ignored former sins without punishment.

Romans 3:23-25 AMP

Many messages from the pulpit today focus on the physical needs of the sheep instead of the spiritual inheritance through the cross of Christ. In my opinion, it is the same as trading our birthright for a bowl of stew. This is the reason so many people are suffering from sickness and disease.

The power over the devil is from a spiritual rebirth and supernatural power of the Holy Spirit. Christ defeated the devil on an empty stomach, and those who follow His example will live in victory on the earth.

I discovered through fasting that life begins "in" Jesus at the new birth. He lives in the Father and sent the Holy Spirit to show us all things.

*... and the Comforter, the Holy Spirit, whom the Father will send in my name, he **will teach you all things, and remind you of all things that I said to you.*** *Not only Need Jesus to Save us from Adamic Sin/Iniquity to be Redeemed*

John 14:26 YNG

It would have been impossible for Jesus to show His disciples the spiritual realm while living in the flesh. The same is true today. Our physical nature is trained at birth to respond to our five senses. The only solution for breaking the grip of the material world is fasting.

Therefore, it was imperative for Jesus to leave and introduce His disciples to the most important liaison between Himself and His Father and the Holy Spirit. The more time they could spend with Him, the sooner they would understand His words and purpose in the flesh.

The spiritual realm and His words below make sense to those who are immersed in His Spirit.

*At that time [**when that day comes**] you will know [for yourselves] that I am in My Father, and you [are] in Me, and I [am] in you.*

John 14:20 AMP

That day came for me when I began to fast. The power over sin, unforgiveness, depression, demonic influence, sickness and death is found inside the resurrection life of Christ. That is not a cliché but the reality of those who have no trust in the physical world and demonstrate it through fasting and prayer.

Jesus never told the devil He was the Son of God. The devil heard God say it at the river Jordan.

And when Jesus had been baptized, just as he came up from the water, suddenly the heavens were opened to him and he saw the Spirit of God descending like a dove and alighting on him.

And a voice from heaven said, This is my Son, the Beloved, with whom I am well pleased.

Matthew 3:16-17 NKJV

Satan was the ruler of both the second heaven (invisible realm) and the heavens of this world (visible worlds) prior to Jesus' resurrection. The devil knew his empire was coming to an end when God announced His Son's priesthood at the river Jordan.

And the seventy came back with joy, saying, Lord, even the evil spirits are under our power in your name.

He said to them, I watched Satan fall from heaven like a lightning flash.

Luke 10-18 HCSBS

Then I heard a loud voice in heaven saying, "Now God's salvation has come! Now God has shown his power as King! Now his Messiah has shown his authority! For the one who stood before our God and accused believers day and night has been thrown out of heaven.

Revelation 12:10 TEV

Fundamental changes occur in a person's beliefs and behavior when they enter a lifestyle of fasting. Quantum fasting exposes our organism to the reality of the invisible world, creating a totally different perspective of Christ and His blood.

The blood is a key spiritual element, which connects heaven and earth to our creator. God designed water and blood as the conduit back to Himself. These life-giving elements carry the DNA of our heavenly Father, and once the Holy Spirit sanctifies us, it will lead us to the mysteries of His Kingdom.

SECTION IV

THE HOLY SPIRIT AND BLOOD

One of the most difficult things to understand is that our physical world is not how it appears. Quantum physics has demonstrated that the building blocks of the material world consist of atoms that are mostly empty space.

The atoms closely resemble hovering clouds of electromagnetic dust. The field of energy around each cloud is composed of an invisible shell of electrons. These clouds of atoms are empty spaces in a material world, but collectively they attract and oppose one another to appear solid.

In other words, the material world that science studies and in which we live is fully dependent on perception. The solidity of objects and matter itself depends on how we observe them, not the particles themselves.

Fasting has been the single greatest tool for destroying my preconceived ideas and perceptions formed from other people's opinions and theories.
The section you are about to read is best understood after beginning a lifestyle of fasting. The illusions of this world are exposed and destroyed through prolonged time spent in the presence of the Holy Spirit.

Before God spoke the material world into existence, it was

necessary to position the Holy Spirit over the water. The three—Father, Son and Holy Spirit—work in unity, in and outside of time, throughout all dimensions, to create order.

In the beginning God created the heavens and the earth.

Now the earth was formless and empty, darkness covered the surface of the watery depths, and the Spirit of God was hovering over the surface of the waters.

Genesis 1:1-2 HCBS

*The angel said to her, "The Holy Spirit will come upon you, and the power of the Most High will **overshadow you;** therefore the child to be born will be holy; he will be called Son of God.*

Luke 1:35 NRSV

The same positioning was necessary before Jesus could be birthed through Mary. Imagine the Holy Spirit hovering over Mary the same way He did in Genesis over the water. God speaks through Gabriel and His living Word is made flesh.

And the Word became flesh and lived among us, and we have seen his glory, the glory as of a father's only son, full of grace and truth.

John 1:14 NRSV

I believe He implanted the blood of almighty God into the

physical world through the womb of Mary. Jesus was the "last" Adam carrying spiritual life in the Father's blood back to all who would repent. Those who believe that Jesus is merely flesh and blood from earth do not understand His blood inheritance or the true purpose of His physical appearance.

After Jesus was pierced below the heart on the cross, water separated from His blood, signifying the physical man, Jesus, was dead. But the God-man would be resurrected to redeem man. His Father's blood reestablished His Kingdom.

And to Jesus by whom the new agreement has been made between God and man, and to the sign of the blood, which says better things than Abel's blood.

Hebrews 12:24 BBE

The mysteries of the universe will always remain hidden from the minds of those whose hearts have not been converted. However, the Holy Spirit will help all who fast to understand the amazing secrets of His kingdom.

If fasting has revealed anything to me, it is my ignorance concerning the most basic principles of life. It was a shock to discover that most of what I had been taught or taken for granted was either wrong or incomplete at best.

Fasting is a key for expanding both our physical and spiritual understanding. The physiological effects on our bodies are scientifically proven, but the spiritual world requires the guidance and direction from the Holy Spirit.

Quantum fasting is the avenue to change our senseless religious speculations and vain imaginations into a meaningful relationship with Christ.

This is he that came by water and blood, even Jesus Christ; not by water only, but by water and blood. And it is the Spirit that beareth witness, because the Spirit is truth.

*For there are three that bear record in heaven, the Father, the Word, and the **Holy Ghost:** and these three are one.*

*And there are three that bear witness in earth, the Spirit, and the water, and the **blood:** and these three agree in one.*

1 John 5:6-8 KJV

Man is a triune being—spirit, soul and body. Therefore, God is Lord over each area and, as such, provides the perfect model in heaven to be manifested on earth.

When we examine the Godhead in heaven with the elements on earth, we discover an interesting correlation. God the Father, the Word and the Holy Spirit manifest on earth as the Spirit, water and blood, respectively.

Jesus is the "living water" of God as well as the creator of the material world. I believe that John strategically connects the spiritual and physical dimensions together with the heavenly components of water and blood.

My book, Immersed in Him, explains the connection between the natural water and Jesus. Creation and the verses in 1 John 5 illustrate the Godhead's unity and power to manifest heaven on earth.

Living immersed in Christ is the mystery that changes our perception from the future to the present. That requires drinking from Christ daily and offering the same refreshment to a dying world.

Jesus answered her, Everyone who drinks of this water will thirst again, but whoever drinks of the water that I will give him will never thirst again; but the water that I will give him will become in him a well of water springing up to eternal life.

John 4:13-14 WEB

CHAPTER 10

THE BLOOD OF THE FIRST AND LAST ADAM

This is He who came by water and blood—Jesus Christ; not only by water, but by water and blood. And it is the Spirit who bears witness, because the Spirit is truth.

1 John 5:6 NKJ

The plan of redemption was prepared and completed by Jesus before the foundation of the world. He was made flesh, in order to return the sinless blood of His Father back to earth to redeem mankind.

The devil was not afraid of anyone born of water from this planet but was terrified of the one who would come with the blood of royalty to overthrow his rule.

God told him in the Garden that his head would be bruised.

I will make you and the woman hate each other; her offspring and yours will always be enemies. Her offspring will crush your head, and you will bite her offspring's heel.

Genesis 3:15 GW

Sin contaminated God's redemptive blood that was placed inside of Adam and resulted in the first murder of his offspring. Moreover, aside from the animals and eight persons on the Ark, everything on the earth was cursed and destroyed by water.

God determined that sin would destroy His universe after only ten generations. The imaginations and lusts of men had reached into the second heaven and resulted in giants populating on the earth.

When people had spread all over the world, and daughters were being born, some of the heavenly beings saw that these young women were beautiful, so they took the ones they liked.

Then the LORD said, I will not allow people to live forever; they are mortal. From now on they will live no longer than 120 years.

In those days, and even later, there were giants on the earth who were descendants of human women and the heavenly beings. They were the great heroes and famous men of long ago.

When the LORD saw how wicked everyone on earth was and how evil their thoughts were all the time, he was sorry that he had ever made them and put them on the earth.

He was so filled with regret that he said, "I will wipe out these people I have created, and also the animals and the birds, because I am sorry that I made any of them."

"But the LORD was pleased with Noah."

Genesis 6:1-8 TEV

Little is understood about the earth before the flood but my speculation is that man had spiritual authority in the second heavens because Adam walked with God. I believe that Adam had the ability to live in both the material and spiritual world simultaneously, as Jesus did.

Adam's sin corrupted the DNA for all mankind and polluted heaven's blood that was coursing through his veins. Sin is a spiritual virus that destroys the soul and body of man. The only cure for that disease is a heavenly transfusion of God's blood.

Jesus crushed the head of satan but not before the devil deposited his poison of pride into the blood of all Adam's descendants.

Now the serpent was more subtle than any **beast** *of the field, which the LORD God had made: and he said to the woman, Yea, hath God said, Ye shall not eat of every tree of the garden?*

Genesis 3:1 WEB

God rescued man from his wrong choice, but his sin had consequences. Satan had a legal right to the soul of man because of the poison, or mark, deposited into the DNA of man.

I believe that to be the mark spoken of in the book of Revelation.

*And the first went, and let what was in his vessel come down on the earth; and it became an **evil poisoning** wound on the men who had the mark of the beast, and who gave worship to his image.*

Revelation 16:2 BBE

Beginning that day, man would be required to choose whom he would serve. The poison from the serpent anesthetized the spirit of man and contaminated his blood, resulting in evil thoughts. He was condemned to believe only what his senses could detect and had no contact with the spiritual world of God.

And the eyes of them both were opened, and they knew that they were naked; and they sewed fig-leaves together, and made themselves aprons.

Genesis 3:7 ASV

Nevertheless, God is faithful to all who call upon Him, and when Adam chose to confess his condition, God forgave him. God sacrificed animals for Adam and his wife, foreshadowing the power of the blood and what was required for man's redemption until Jesus would manifest as the spotless lamb for all mankind.

GOD made leather clothing for Adam and his wife and dressed them.

Genesis 3:21 The Message

The plan of God was to reproduce "Sons" through Adam to rule and reign on earth as it is in the heavens. That plan was accomplished through Jesus, the last Adam.

So also it is written, The first man Adam became a living soul. The last Adam became a life-giving spirit.

1 Corinthians 15:45 ASV

Those who study the scriptures understand that God used Abraham as the bloodline to birth Jesus. God protected, blessed and multiplied the Israelites because of His covenant with Abraham and redemptive plans for the human race.

The goal of the devil was to corrupt the bloodline of Christ with sin, thereby preventing God from redeeming man.

Our blood is the legal right the devil has to control our thoughts and lives. The only way back to the Father is through a blood transfusion at the cross of Christ. Without His blood, our mind and thoughts will be controlled by the devil.

Jesus was born on earth, as the Son of Man, to return God's redemptive blood to man. The DNA from the Father, which was polluted by Adam's sin, would return as the "spotless Lamb." God had to sacrifice His Son for the same purpose that He killed the animal to redeem Adam's sin.

The righteous blood of God entered earth through the body of Jesus and reopened heaven to man. Jesus is not only the physical life source, but also the bridge into the spiritual realm.

Jesus understood the power and purpose of the Holy Spirit and rebuked those who did not honor Him. **The Holy Spirit is the guardian of God's blood and offers redemption to those God draws.**

People cannot come to me unless the Father who sent me draws them to me; and I will raise them to life on the last day.

John 6:44 TEV

I assure you that people can be forgiven all their sins and all the evil things they may say.

But whoever says evil things against the Holy Spirit will never be forgiven, because he has committed an eternal sin.

Mark 3:28-29 TEV

Jesus never defended Himself but was very quick to warn anyone who spoke against the precious Holy Spirit. Those of you who have been acquainted with Him understand our Lord's zeal.

After everyone leaves and you feel all alone, the Holy Spirit is still by your side whispering words of encouragement and love. The depths of His love are unsearchable because He is from the heart of the Father.

Each experience with the Holy Spirit has shown me something new about His heart and creation. Every encounter has altered my understanding of His ways and designs. He continues to give me greater insights into the heart of God.

The world of God is not accessible through the physical senses, but it is tangible and visible to those who learn certain principles. Our spirit must be alive to the Holy Spirit in order to understand that realm.

Those who fast often will become very familiar with Him, because when it feels like hell is swallowing you, **the voice of the Holy Spirit will tame your thoughts and still your emotions.**

God breathed into the nose of Adam to create life. Breathing through our nose oxygenates the blood 10 to 15 times more than breathing through our mouth. Science is unable to discover the power that ignites blood, which perpetually produces life in our bodies.

I believe the Holy Spirit was the life force that was breathed into Adam the same way Jesus breathed on His disciples when He returned from destroying the rule of satan.

Then he breathed on them and said, Receive the Holy Spirit.

John 20:22 TEV

The breath from Jesus was the same that activated the first Adam and now activated the new blood covenant He had made. This time the Holy Spirit could protect the covenant and His blood from contamination because Jesus crushed the serpent's head through His perfect sacrifice and victory over death.

Man still has the right to choose sin over righteousness, but never again can his unrighteous choice pollute the redemptive fountain formed in heaven through Christ's sacrifice.

CHAPTER 11

BLOOD AND THOUGHTS

For I am conscious of my thoughts about you, says the Lord, thoughts of peace and not of evil, to give you hope at the end.

Jeremiah 29:11 YNG

The origins of thoughts have been the source of debate and research for centuries. Science calls thoughts everything from energy to chemical reactions by the brain.

The truth can always be found in God's word because He is the author of all things. Thoughts began inside God before the foundation of the world. God has never stopped sending good thoughts toward His creations.

We know that His thoughts are hindered before man receives them. Otherwise, the world would be a different place. The following scripture in Isaiah helps us understand the responsibility of man in order to obtain His goodness.

*Let the wicked leave their way of life **and change their way of thinking.** Let them turn to the LORD, our God; he is merciful and quick to forgive.*

***My thoughts, says the LORD, are not like yours,** and my ways are different from yours.*

Isaiah 55:7-8 TEV

Man must consciously change the way he thinks and turn his receiver towards God. It is important to note that God does not say man cannot think like Him, just not in his current condition. The first step is to repent, which is changing the way one thinks.

Repentance is not emotionally feeling sorry for wrongdoing but rather a complete restructuring of mentality. The only one capable of rebuilding our mind is the Holy Spirit.

That is precisely why Jesus said, "REPENT," for the kingdom of heaven is at hand. Repent means to CHANGE THE WAY ONE THINKS. No one is capable of entering the kingdom of God with the same mentality or corrupted blood. That is why there must be a new birth.

*Nor will they say, Look, here it is or There for indeed, **the kingdom of God is in your midst.***

Luke 17:21 NET

The spiritual world operates differently from the physical. God's kingdom surrounds us, but our mentality and thoughts produced from the blood of Adam prevents our believing or hearing Jesus. Those born from the Spirit have their Father's DNA, and all things are different.

I correct and punish everyone I love. **So make up your minds** *to turn away from your sins.*

Listen! I am standing and knocking at your door. If you hear my voice and open the door, I will come in and we will eat together.

Revelation 3:19-20 CEV

Blood is the life force of man and, I believe, originated in heaven from the heart of God. It is my opinion that the Holy Spirit is the blood of God and assigned to redeem those whose lives belong to Christ.

Moreover, the blood, because of its origin provides not only physical life, but spiritual life as well. The blood and mind work together to form ideas, imaginations and thoughts. If the mind has not been "renewed" through Christ, the thoughts will produce sin, sickness and eventual death in the body.

And be renewed in the spirit of your minds,

Ephesians 4:23 NAB

Now the natural person does not accept what pertains to the Spirit of God, for to him it is foolishness, and he cannot understand it, because it is judged spiritually.

The spiritual person, however, can judge everything but is not subject to judgment by anyone.

For "who has known the mind of the Lord, so as to counsel him?" But we have the mind of Christ.

1 Corinthians 2:14-16 NAB

For example, if a farmer plants good seeds into properly watered ground, it will produce a healthy harvest. If, on the other hand, the ground is not prepared and he does not keep the weeds and birds away, the harvest will be destroyed.

Therefore, if the blood remains lawless because of the first Adam's transgression, the soil of our mind will not produce good thoughts. Furthermore, the thoughts formed from sin will eventually destroy both the soul and body.

And he said, What have you done? the voice of your brother's blood is crying to me from the earth.

Genesis 4:10 BBE

And to Jesus the negotiator of a new Covenant, and to the sprinkled blood which speaks in more gracious tones than that of Abel.

Hebrews 12:24 Weymouth

In other words, **the blood from heaven has a different frequency from the blood of those who have never repented.** Our thoughts will magnetically attract the vibration it is tuned to receive. The power of His blood will attract the goodness of God and life everlasting.

The baptism in the Holy Spirit is more than speaking in tongues; it is the immersion in the blood of Christ. The power in that act is the fire that purifies our blood and transforms our minds.

*I indeed baptize you with water unto repentance, but He who is coming after me is mightier than I, whose sandals I am not worthy to carry. **He will baptize you with the Holy Spirit and fire.***

Matthew 3:11 NKJV

Are you starting to receive a deeper revelation of the "baptism of the Holy Spirit"? One of the most important aspects of the baptism is changing our thoughts and quality of blood. **Fasting is the fastest way to change your blood in order to prepare for the infilling of His.**

If our spirit is not connected to the Holy Spirit, our desires will be from the flesh. I believe food plays a role along with water and oxygen to equip our bodies and maintain the quality of our blood. Fasting has shown me many things about our bodies and its relationship with food. If one will make fasting a lifestyle, the choices of food will change.

Unless one is immersed in the blood of heaven through a divine transfusion, our minds will not think about the things of heaven. One may "feel" different, but an unchanged mind will eventually control the emotions and prevent access from the Holy Spirit.

Those who attempt to change their thoughts without the baptism of Christ and His wilderness experiences may achieve temporary results but will not activate the everlasting changes of the Holy Spirit for their lives.

The majestic wisdom of God is cloaked in perpetually changing dimensions to provoke our passion for Him and destroy the devil's hold on our mentality.

In other words, the presence of God must be the primary pursuit of our life. Otherwise, the devil will continue to control our thoughts. For example, if one stops viewing pornography or taking drugs because of religious shame, the same person will usually begin another destructive behavior because they have not understood the root cause of their desires.

Unless our spirit and soul are submerged in the Holy Spirit, our blood will continue to affect our thinking. The unredeemed mind is an open door for the devil to control our emotions and desires. If the doors are not shut, the enemy will use one's unchanged thinking to create complacency or dogmatic doctrines. Examples of this are found throughout church history.

In every move of God, denominations are formed around the preconceived belief that they have the only relevant revelation of Christ. Remember when John told Jesus, "We saw someone casting out demons in your name?"

John said to Jesus, Teacher, we saw someone forcing demons out of a person by using the power and authority of your name. We tried to stop him because he was not one of us.

Mark 9:38 GW

They wanted to stop him because he was not part of "their" group. This is precisely why the "Body of Christ" requires the head or mind of Christ to function as one.

The origin of our thoughts must be from the blood of Christ. Otherwise, our past memories and associations will corrupt the outcome. Man's fall should remind each of us that we have the final choice in what we believe and think.

CHAPTER 12

THE DEMONIC AND
OUR THINKING

The person who lives a sinful life belongs to the devil, because the devil has been committing sin since the beginning. The reason that the Son of God appeared was to destroy what the devil does.

1 John 3:8 GW

He who is habitually guilty of sin is a child of the Devil, because the Devil has been a sinner from the very beginning. The Son of God appeared for the purpose of undoing the work of the Devil.

1 John 3:8 Weymouth

Separate from but of 2 powers

[But] he who commits sin [who practices evildoing] is of the devil [takes his character from the evil one], for the devil has sinned (violated the divine law) from the beginning. The reason the Son of God was made manifest (visible) was to undo (destroy, loosen, and dissolve) the works the devil [has done].

1 John 3:8 AMP

Each translation of the verse implies Jesus destroyed the "work" of the devil and that is why He manifested in the flesh. But unless the church understands what John meant by "work," there will be limited victory over sin. Therefore, when people sin, it indicates they have not understood the "work" Jesus destroyed.

Satan uses deception and doubt to create unbelief inside the minds and hearts of each person. The power over sin is spiritual, and it cannot be understood from an unredeemed mind. Sin is the nature of rebellion found in the character of the devil. Those whose minds have not been washed in the blood of Christ will be deceived.

The hypnotic trance perpetrated by the devil over the inhabitants of the world is the "work" Jesus destroyed. He ended man's captivity by taking the fear of death captive. Nevertheless, if people trust fear more than faith, they will live their life as a slave to sin.

We have just described that the power of the devil is through fear. He is the master illusionist who alters shadows and light to reflect fear into the minds and hearts of those he has traumatized in life.

We all have experienced situations in our lives, which have scarred or frightened us. It was during that split second of vulnerability the devil planted a seed of doubt and unbelief inside our hearts. The seed is nourished each time we experience fear or think about things contrary to God's goodness.

For example, as children during summer vacations we would play outside until late at night. Hide and Seek was the most popular game we played. The one who managed to stay undiscovered while others searched was the winner.

On one occasion, we hid inside a magnificent two-story vacant house. We all knew it was wrong to go inside, but the adventure of entering the forbidden territory was too much to resist. Besides, we were kids, and as long as we didn't break anything, we believed we could talk our way out of any trouble.

With our imaginations running wild, we explored every room in the house. Finally, each of us found a place to hide and waited to be discovered. It seemed I had been hiding for a long time, so I decided to look around for the others. When I opened the door to look downstairs, I felt something touch my arm. Spinning around I saw this figure dressed in a white gown standing behind me. Later, I learned the person dressed up was one of my playmates.

To say I was scared would be an understatement. The fear that passed through my body caused my heart to beat wildly, as my mind created all types of terrible thoughts. I ran out as fast as my feet would carry me until I heard the others laughing loudly at my reactions.

What seemed like a harmless prank opened my heart and mind to spiritual seeds of fear, which is the poison from the beast in the Garden. Fear produces an atmosphere of doubt and unbelief and is the soil from which illusions and suggestions prosper.

The instant the heart is gripped with fear, the devil will control our thoughts with panic. Regardless of the situation, the mind will focus on doom and gloom as the eventual outcome.

The work of the devil is to create a perpetual fountain of doubt and unbelief bubbling inside the hearts and minds of people, activated by images of fear. Each time he succeeds at frightening or intimidating someone, he has created a hyperlink or instant connection to that person's psyche for future activation.

Future panic and terror in a person is as simple as activating the link or picture from a past trauma. Once activated, those images will control that person's behavior.

In essence, most people are easily manipulated with images from past traumas whose origin is fear. The pain of divorce generally creates serious problems for future relationships between men and women. In most cases, walls of resentment and mistrust are constructed from the pain. Consequently, the obstacle becomes a memorial to fear, doubt and mistrust and will ultimately be the construction site for future images of pain and suffering. Moreover, if one experiences pain, the mind will retrieve those images and relive them as if they just occurred.

Behaviors are more easily manipulated when people are selfish. A person's character must be within the laws of righteousness, or they will be positioned for deception.

We have heard or read stories of Christians who in "moments of weakness" committed tragic sins, destroying their ministries and families. Most sins are the result of submitting to thoughts constructed from desires, whose primary purpose is self. If our minds are unfamiliar with the spiritual realm, our bodies will be an open door for unclean spirits.

Everyone is tempted by his own desires as they lure him away and trap him.

Then desire becomes pregnant and gives birth to sin. When sin grows up, it gives birth to death.

James 1:14-15 GW

Demonic influence begins in the form of thoughts until one surrenders their will to the suggestions. The manifestation of selfish thoughts in the material world creates the legal right for the habitation of the unclean spirits.

Some churches avoid deliverance ministry because of the fear that people will be worse off. That position may have been formed from not understanding Luke 11:26. We will examine that scripture from another perspective.

The unclean spirit, when he has gone out of a man, goes through dry places, looking for rest; and when he does not get it, he says, I will go back to my house from which I came.

And when he comes, he sees that it has been made fair and clean. Then he goes and gets seven other spirits more evil than himself, and they go in, and take their places there: and the last condition of that man is worse than the first.

Luke 11:24-26 BBE

After an evil spirit is removed from a person, it receives the same torment the human soul does without God. The spirit of man is the life source for man and, as such, provides life even for demons.

The understanding of the spiritual realm is essential and is the promise to those who are truly born of the "water" (quotation marks added) and Spirit of God. The words spoken to Nicodemus by Jesus in John 3 are not symbolic terms.

Jesus answered, Verily, verily, I say unto thee, Except one be born of water and the Spirit, he cannot enter into the kingdom of God!

John 3:5 ASV

The kingdom of God is the power and authority over all creatures in both the visible and invisible world. Angels and demons reside outside the material world, but unclean spirits require a physical host to survive. Angels, on the other hand, are sustained by God's glory and are sent to serve the saints chosen before the foundation of the world.

Man is approximately 70% water because Jesus is the "living water" both spiritually and physically. Furthermore, ALL things have their existence and being through Jesus.

And He Himself existed before all things, and in Him all things consist (cohere, are held together).

Colossians 1:17 AMP

Therefore, once an unclean spirit is separated from a person or physical host, it desperately searches for water in the form of another physical host. Their manifestation requires the water of this world in the form of man. It is the combination of water and Spirit, which is the source of all things.

The devil and his kingdom know that Jesus is the origin and source of all life, but their treason has blinded them eternally. They exist because of God's will and are permitted to do what God or we allow. The unclean spirits go through dry places looking for rest, which is only found in Christ.

Man's physical life expectancy is limited. Therefore, unclean spirits must contaminate entire families' bloodlines, commonly referred to as generational curses, in order to sustain themselves. It is common among family gatherings to hear heartbreaking stories surrounding premature deaths, insanity, adultery, suicides and others.

Many of us are familiar with immediate family members who have struggled with everything from drug and sexual abuse to cancer and heart disease. These are clear indications of unclean spirits occupying family members from one generation to the next. One of the keys for maintaining our freedom from demonic influence is found in the following scripture:

As He thus spoke a woman in the crowd called out in a loud voice, Blessed is the mother who carried you, and the breasts that you have sucked.

Nay rather, He replied, they are blessed who hear God's Message and carefully keep it.

Luke 11:27-28 Weymouth

Once a person is delivered from demonic influence, whether it be addictions or diseases, the power over that situation belongs to those the Lord has set free.

For example, those persons taking medication or prescription drugs because of a doctor's diagnosis will be very diligent to follow his instructions. By the same token those who have been delivered by "Doctor" Jesus must follow His prescription, which is to be led by His Spirit.

Unfortunately, most people are unaware that sickness, diseases, drug addictions and oppressions are spiritual in nature and thus require the leading of the Holy Spirit to be set free. Paul makes it clear in his letters the necessity for depending on the Spirit of God.

For as many as are led by the Spirit of God, these are children of God.

Romans 8:14 WEB

If your spiritual nature is your guide, you are not subject to Moses' laws.

Galatians 5:18 GW

The Spirit has given us life; he must also control our lives.

Galatians 5:25 TEV

It is very interesting that even unclean spirits understand degrees of evil. Remember, the scripture says, **and then he goes and gets seven other spirits more evil than himself.**

The only difference between the mentality in the visible and invisible world is the physical body. The soul represents the sum total of a person's life while living in the physical world.

In other words, if the soul does not surrender to the Spirit of God, he or she will serve their ideas and beliefs formed from their senses.

Therefore, the beliefs of the soul will be the same in the body or outside of it. The only difference will be the location of the soul after the body dies.

Don't be afraid of those who kill the body but cannot kill the soul. Instead, fear the one who can destroy both body and soul in hell.

Matthew 10:28 GW

And the dust returneth to the earth as it was, And the spirit returneth to God who gave it.

Ecclesiastes 12:7 YNG

These scriptures indicate God as the final resting place for man's spirit and the earth for his body. But the final home of man's soul is determined by the choices each person makes while living in the material world. The soul must be surrendered to the Holy Spirit in order to win that battle. Otherwise, the devil will control the mind with doubt, unbelief and emotions.

The mind believes lies and forms its reality from that position. If we do not change our thinking, we will live forever in darkness.

Those whose mind is filled with darkness on earth attract like-minded souls. The demonic realm is an atmosphere of chaos and fear created by wrong thinking.

After the soul is separated from the spirit it is tormented forever by the demons it once entertained through fear and wrong thinking. God ultimately determines the level of torment.

Love alters our thoughts by exposing our minds to light. Jesus is the source of all light, love and salvation. Love exposes the enemy and illuminates the darkness. Fear has no substance in the light.

There is no fear in love; perfect love drives out all fear. So then, love has not been made perfect in anyone who is afraid, because fear has to do with punishment.

1 John 4:18 TEV

Jesus spoke to the Pharisees again. He said, "I am the light of the world. Whomever follows Me will have a life filled with light and will never live in the dark."

John 8:12 GW

Jesus is speaking about the difference between the visible and invisible worlds or physical and spiritual dimensions. This is clear because the majority of people live in areas that have darkness.

Life was created in the light of God. Sin corrupts the light with impure or distorted thoughts, like filters used by cinematographers to change the quality of light on the image they are filming.

The likeness or figure is the same, but the light is altered or shadowed, which changes the appearance on the film or movie screen.

The purity of our thoughts is governed by the source and frequency of the light. Thoughts are a type of lens over the mind's eye. Christ is the light of life, but if our minds are corrupted by wrong thoughts, fear will be the result and we will live in darkness.

But if your eye is evil, your whole body will be full of darkness.

If therefore the light that is in you is darkness, how great is the darkness.

Matthew 6:23 WEB

The precious Holy Spirit continually orchestrates events in the natural world to awaken us to God's mercy and grace. I believe **grace is a spiritual force that absorbs darkness long enough for our spirit to experience the Light of Christ. The acknowledgement of that event opens our spirit to more grace.**

Because ***by grace you have salvation through faith;*** *and that not of yourselves: it is given by God:*

Ephesians 2:8 BBE

Do not let all kinds of strange teachings lead you from the right way. It is good ***to receive inner strength from God's grace, and not by obeying rules about foods;*** *those who obey these rules have not been helped by them.*

Hebrews 13:9 TEV

The work of Christ fulfilled the law, allowing grace to soften our hearts and minds in order to receive the truth, in the person of Jesus. Today, He resides in the hearts and minds of those who choose the Holy Spirit and the unseen world as the reality, instead of the physical world.

Therefore, those whose lives are spent following Jesus in the natural world will live in God's invisible world forever.

For the law was given through Moses. Grace and truth came through Jesus Christ.

John 1:17 WEB

He who loves his life will lose it, and he who hates his life in this world will keep it for eternal life.

John 12:25 NKJV

SECTION V

THE SOUL

Awesome chapter!!

Quantum fasting will produce the greatest results in our soul, which is why, the devil fights desperately to prevent the Body of Christ from participating. Once fasting became a lifestyle in my life, my thoughts and physical health took a quantum leap in divine revelation and health.

It gave me the power to subdue my soul and train it not to submit to the doubts and unbelief of the devil. The heavenly tool of fasting will destroy the strongholds, which the soul has created from fear. The model of dominion promised in Genesis will again become the birthright for you and your family.

*Then God said, **Let Us make man in Our image, according to Our likeness;** let them have dominion over the fish of the sea, over the birds of the air, and over the cattle, over all the earth and over every creeping thing that creeps on the earth.*

Genesis 1:26 NKJV

God made man according to his own species and provided him with a soul, which separates him from the angels and animals. The soul is the instrument designed to work in conjunction with the spirit to manifest heaven on earth.

Jesus was the perfect example of a soul completely submitted to His spirit. The result was the manifestation of the Kingdom of God everywhere He traveled.

The command to dominate the creatures on the earth requires governmental understanding. The power of rulership on the earth eventually extends to the heavens.

Do you not know that the saints will judge the world? And, if the world will be judged by you, are you unworthy to judge the smallest matters?

Do you not know that we shall judge angels? How much more, things that pertain to this life?

1 Corinthians 6:3-4 NKJV

The soul is designed for planetary rulership and judgment. But, if it is not connected to the Creator, the results will be the conditions of the world that we see today.

Instead of ruling angels and worlds, man is preoccupied with material pursuits that offer little eternal value. The blood of Christ is the soul's only resource, which will join his spirit to the Spirit of God. This is the only connection that will convert the soul and mind of man.

This Son of God is Jesus Christ, who came by water and blood. He didn't come with water only, but with water and with blood.

The Spirit is the one who verifies this, because the Spirit is the truth.

1 John 5:6 BBE

This is important to understand, because Jesus was not only God's Son but also the Son of man, in order for His sinless sacrifice to be counted righteous for all men. The blood He shed for our redemption was from His Father, and the water represents the basic component for all material life, including man.

These two elements are key for those who want to experience the depths of the invisible Kingdom of God manifested through quantum fasting. The devil is afraid of those who are born of both water and spirit through His blood, because they are the heirs of God.

The senses, intellect, emotions and beliefs are located in our soul. It is the soul that provides man with the capacity to experience the wonders of God in both dimensions. The government of man resides in his soul, which is exercised each time he makes decisions. God designed man's soul to govern both the visible and invisible worlds, starting with his thoughts. The ultimate choice one makes between trusting God or self determines the soul's eternal home.

"Do you not believe, Philip, that I am in the Father and the Father is in me?

The words that I have spoken to you," Jesus said to his disciples, "Do not come from me. The Father, who remains in me, does his own work."

Believe me when I say that I am in the Father and the Father is in me. If not, believe because of the things I do.

I am telling you the truth: those who believe in me will do what I do—yes, they will do even greater things, because I am going to the Father.

John 14:10-12 TEV

Jesus asked Philip if he believed Him. This is the question always answered by one's soul. The creator of all things resided on the inside of Jesus, invisible to His disciples.

Here is an example to illustrate this powerful truth: Astronauts wear space suits when walking in outer space to protect themselves and to provide them with oxygen. If they were to rescue someone in outer space, would it be because of the spacesuit or the man inside? The man inside the suit was the hero, but the action required the protective gear.

Jesus was telling Philip to trust the invisible person inside Him, because He is the source of life and miracles. Jesus was the body and soul of His Father who did the work.
This trust is determined by the information processed from our mind and soul, and it forms our belief system. The environment is a major factor for influencing what a person believes. For

example, if a person only watches TV and listens to the news, their belief system will be decidedly different from those who fast and pray. Therefore, if the visible world is the main resource for determing what one believes, that person will not do the greater works Jesus told Philip about.

Quantum scientists affirm what Solomon said by the Holy Spirit thousands of years ago. Our heart produces the reality we think about the most. Consequently, the source of our thoughts produces the life we lead.

For as he thinketh in his soul, so is he.

Proverbs 23:7a Darby

For as he thinks in his heart, so is he.

Proverbs 23:7a NKJV

Quantum fasting opens the door of heaven, empowering man's spirit to control his soul and body. It is the most powerful tool I have discovered for changing the way I think. This is the first step to altering our beliefs and exposing our minds to the limitless possibilities IN CHRIST.

The word of God is alive and active, sharper than any double-edged sword.
It cuts all the way through, to where soul and spirit meet, to where joints and marrow come together.

It judges the desires and thoughts of the heart.

Hebrews 4:12 TEV

Jesus said, "Anything is possible if you can believe." Jesus is the master of everything that is, was and will be. Think of that! Everything that ever will be or has been was completed IN CHRIST! The soul has the ability to understand the reality of that statement and the joy contained in "knowing" the author of it all, Christ.

The soul is veiled in darkness from birth, and unless one's spirit can be awakened, it will form its reality from the material world. That darkness is sin, which is the substance produced from a corrupted mentality. Once sin is removed through repentance, one can experience love, which is a frequency from heaven.

As we discussed before, **the heart of man in union with the source of love can change the material world and alter our perceptions of reality and the way we think. Fasting is by far the most effective method in achieving this transformation.**

Those who fast often will experience new understanding about the scriptures and their assignments from before the foundation of the world. God is the Father of all spirits. In my opinion, one of the goals of the Holy Spirit is to remind each spirit of their origin with their Father before becoming a living soul.

If you are reading this book, most likely your spirit is longing for the relationship it enjoyed with the Father before the foundation of the world. I believe the Holy Spirit has been assigned to fulfill that desire. He will never force you, but He does love you enough to use every method possible to reach you.

The Holy Spirit was sent to remind us through His Word about the reality of the invisible world. The Word is Jesus and He is the author of both the visible and invisible dimension. God is Spirit, and the Word He spoke in Genesis contains everything that was and is and will be.

Often during a fast, the Holy Spirit would reveal the relationship between my soul and body. On one occasion, I saw the Mercy Seat sitting at the right hand of the Father in heaven. Jesus is the mercy seat, and His blood is the power whose source is love.

CHAPTER 13

THE MERCY SEAT

The Ark of the Covenant was wood furniture covered in gold inhabited by God and His Word. This is a depiction of Christ in us, the hope of glory.

Jesus is God and the Word made flesh. He must be man in order to be a propitiation for sin. We are created like the ark, in order to carry the supernatural power of God everywhere we go.

And you shall put inside the ark the Testimony [the Ten Commandments], which I will give you.

And you shall make a mercy seat (a covering) of pure gold, two cubits and a half long and a cubit and a half wide.

Exodus 25:16-17 AMP

Jesus suffered the most horrible death at the hands of those who prophesied His coming and salvation. This sacrifice is unmatched in the universe and is what gives Him authority over sin, sickness and death. The Holy Spirit unveiled the picture of the mercy seat when I began to fast for extended periods of time. He showed me this vision outside of time and space, because that was the way it was presented to Moses.

Moses was chosen to implement the vision God gave him during his two consecutive 40 days without food and water. During that time, he was shown, among other things, the ark and mercy seat. God could not trust this vision to anyone who had not died to this world. Fasting is the way to demonstrate one's detachment from this world.

He was given the responsibility to construct a physical manifestation from the invisible realm of eternity. The Tabernacle, along with all of the ordinances of the Law, was part of the redemptive picture of God. Everything from the tent to the candlesticks was a physical representation of Christ and His redemption.

Jesus is the mercy seat and the testimony of life over death through His blood sacrifice.

God showed that Christ is the throne of mercy where God's approval is given through faith in Christ's blood. In his patience God waited to deal with sins committed in the past.

Romans 3:25 GW

God offered him, so that by his blood he should become the means by which people's sins are forgiven through their faith in him. God did this in order to demonstrate that he is righteous. In the past he was patient and overlooked people's sins; but in the present time he deals with their sins, in order to demonstrate his righteousness.

Romans 3:25 TEV

The work of Christ is described in Exodus through the description and design of the ark. It is essential to understand that the guardians over the ark are the same ones set at the entrance of the Garden of Eden to prevent man from living forever in his fallen condition.

Then the LORD God said, "Behold, the man has become like one of Us, to know good and evil. And now, lest he put out his hand and take also of the tree of life, and eat, and live forever"—

So He drove out the man; and He placed cherubim at the east of the garden of Eden, and a flaming sword which turned every way, to guard the way to the tree of life.

Genesis 3:22,24 NKJV

And you shall make two cherubim (winged angelic figures) of [solid] hammered gold on the two ends of the mercy seat. And the cherubim shall spread out their wings above, covering the mercy seat with their wings, facing each other and looking down toward the mercy seat.

Exodus 25:18,20 AMP

The same cherubim assigned to prevent man from entering the Garden are commissioned to usher him into God's presence. They are positioned above the mercy seat in order to rejoice with those who offer their lives to Christ. In heaven it is the highest form of worship and celebrated by heaven's hosts.

Jesus said, "In the same way God's angels are happy when even one person turns to him."

Luke 15:10 CEV

The mercy seat is the place of transparency and the surrendering of our will. This is a place of atonement, which for the Jews meant fasting and repentance.

Our soul's level of sacrifice determines the quality and aroma of our worship. The greater the sacrifice, the sweeter the fragrance and smell in heaven. I believe the fragrance from Noah's sacrifice was an important part of the covenant God made with earth and man forever.

*The odor of the sacrifice pleased the LORD, and he said to himself, "Never again will I put the earth under a curse because of what people do; I know that from the time they are young their thoughts are evil. **Never again will I destroy all living beings, as I have done this time.***

Genesis 8:21 TEV

God designed our physical body as the perfect container for His

Spirit to reside and ultimately convert our souls to heavenly instruments of worship.

Worship alters our physical world and changes our perceptions of reality according to our revelation of Christ.

Everyone must have a personal encounter with Christ in order to know he or she has passed from death unto life. For me, this event occurred after fasting 40 days. God in His infinite wisdom designed a place for man to meet with Him outside church walls, synagogues and temples.

Fasting was the tool I used to prepare myself for this experience. My intimate experience occurred in the timeless eternity above the mercy seat where He taught me how to worship Him.

During that time the Holy Spirit taught me the frequency of heaven and what love sounds like to God. The angels move to the beat of God's heart and the sound of His thoughts. There is nothing on earth that can match the vibrations my soul experienced in heaven.

The power over death is the melody of God's blood on the mercy seat. It is a sound, which terrifies the devil and sets captives free. The music in heaven is the resurrection life in Jesus' blood and it resonates in the outer most regions of the universe.

Those who fast will understand worship from another

perspective and become God's instrument of resurrection on the earth.

CHAPTER 14

OLD WINE SKINS

The word *fast* in Hebrew is tsowm pronounced "tsoom," and it means to *cover or close the mouth*. Moses did not use that word in Exodus or Leviticus but instead used the word *anah*, pronounced "*aw-naw'*."

The root word *anah* means to be afflicted, bowed down, humbled, or meek. Perhaps, this gives us some insight as to why Moses was considered the meekest man on the earth.

Then the disciples of John came to Him, saying, "Why do we and the Pharisees fast often, but Your disciples do not fast?"

And Jesus said to them, "Can the friends of the bridegroom mourn as long as the bridegroom is with them? But the days will come when the bridegroom will be taken away from them, and then they will fast.

Nor do they put new wine into old wineskins, or else the wineskins break, the wine is spilled, and the wineskins are ruined. But they put new wine into new wineskins, and both are preserved."

Matthew 9:14-15,17 NKJV

Wine skins are the vessels made from animal hides, which protect and permit a limited amount of young wine to be portable. The skin was considered old when it had been filled previously with wine, and new wine could not be mixed in the same container without loosing both the wine and skin.

It is my belief that fasting is the process that will supernaturally oil the skin from the inside out, in order for it to receive the new wine of Jesus. The response by Jesus illustrates His contempt for religion and its understanding of fasting.

The union of the Holy Spirit and Jesus will transform our heart into the altar or house of God. Thus, the skin on the outside will be God's tent as it was in the Old Testament.

Fasting will maintain the physical tent while the new wine nourishes the soul and spirit with fresh revelations each day. Fasting is not a religious method to obtain God's approval, but a weapon for dismantling our natures. It is the soul of man that has the greatest need for reconstruction and expansion.

The old wineskin is a container incapable of change or manifesting the revelations of heaven. Christ is both the kingdom of God and the new wine. The new wine sustains our growth and provides perpetual revelation for abiding in the kingdom. The scripture explains the various methods for offering sacrifices on the altar of God. The "drink offering" consisted of wine and was sacrificed along with exact proportions of "cereal and meat offerings." The Old Testament is the type and shadow of Christ whose life was the perfect sacrifice poured out for all men.

The Bible describes Jesus in John 15 as the vine. In order to produce fruit, each of us must abide IN HIM.

I believe the fruit of that vine produces the new wine Jesus is speaking of in Luke 22. Those who want fresh revelation must be connected to Him and even be pruned by God. Pruning provides the sweetest berries.

One of the purposes of fruit is to reproduce and provide health and healing in the bodies of those who consume it. The Father tends the vineyard in order to produce a greater harvest and the best wine.

The greatest future we could have as His fruit is to be chosen and consumed by the Master. Paul recognized the relationship between the drink offering and being chosen as God's fruit.

And even if I am offered like a drink offering, giving myself for the cause and work of your faith, I am glad and have joy with you all.

Philippians 2:17 BBE

For I am already being poured out as a drink offering, and the time of my departure has come.

2 Timothy 2:4 NASB

I think it is important to understand that the Old Testament position of fasting was considered afflicting the soul on the Day of Atonement. The following scriptures describe God's ordinance to the Israelites.

It shall be a statute to you forever that in the seventh month [nearly October] on the tenth day of the month you shall afflict yourselves [by fasting with penitence and humiliation] and do no work at all, either the native-born or the stranger who dwells temporarily among you.

For on this day atonement shall be made for you, to cleanse you; from all your sins you shall be clean before the Lord.

It is a Sabbath of [solemn] rest to you, and you shall afflict yourselves [by fasting with penitence and humiliation]; it is a statute forever.

Leviticus 19:29-31 AMP

And the Lord said to Moses, also the tenth day of this seventh month is the Day of Atonement; it shall be a holy [called] assembly, and you shall afflict yourselves [by fasting in penitence and humility] and present an offering made by fire to the Lord. And you shall do no work on this day, for it is the Day of Atonement, to make atonement for you before the Lord your God.

For whoever is not afflicted [by fasting in penitence and humility] on this day shall be cut off from among his people [that he may not be included in the atonement made for them].

And whoever does any work on that same day I will destroy from among his people.

You shall do no kind of work [on that day]. It is a statute forever throughout your generations in all your dwellings.

It shall be to you a Sabbath of rest, and you shall afflict yourselves [by fasting in penitence and humility]. On the ninth day of the month from evening to evening, you shall keep your Sabbath.

Leviticus 23:26-32 AMP

Religion will always represent the old skin because it is incapable of expanding with an ever-increasing revelation of Christ. Jesus makes the following statement in Matthew to reveal the purposes behind the Mosaic Law.

If you had known what this means: I want mercy and not sacrifice, you would not have condemned the innocent.

Matthew 12:7 NET

Those who drink old wine will become intoxicated on themselves, while judging others. Pride and self-righteousness are the characteristics of those drinking that wine. Sacrifice was the mercy of God on their behalf. In other words, Israel was the old wineskin God was using to carry the promise of new wine. Had they understood the mercy of God, they would have received the new wine Jesus was offering them.

Jacob did something in Genesis after meeting God that illustrates the wine as Jesus and the oil as the Holy Spirit.

And Jacob set up a pillar (monument) in the place where he talked with [God], a pillar of stone; and he poured a drink offering on it and he poured oil on it.

And Jacob called the name of the place where God had talked with him Bethel [house of God].

Genesis 35:14-15 AMP

One will discover that most of the miracles performed by Jesus were done on the Sabbath day. This is significant because, in essence, He was demonstrating Himself as the fulfillment of the Law. Jesus is both the Sabbath and the seventh day in Genesis chapter 2.

Jesus is the physical completion of everything foretold by the prophets throughout the scripture. Religion is so preoccupied with form that it misses the substance.

In other words, the leaders of Jesus' day were more concerned about His birthplace and doctrine than His authority over sin, sickness and death. The same is true today. Fasting is a struggle without a revelation of the invisible world. But the Spirit wants to set you free and will help you every step of the way.

The soul is most accustomed to giving orders and therefore must relinquish that role to the Holy Spirit. The difference between the spiritual and physical world is easy to discern once our spirit is awakened.

Fasting is the designated tool God will use to perform the most thorough work. The soul and mind are the most resistant to change and are the biggest challenge for man.

Those who choose to fast will be faced with difficult decisions that will require perseverance to overcome. Nevertheless, one who will spend hours in prayer and worship will succeed. The power released in fasting separates us from physical appetites and introduces us to the world of faith.

Fasting is capable of transforming the soul from pride to humility, but the battle will be fierce and terrifying at the beginning. The mind is the soul's companion in self-protection and will steadfastly manifest danger signs throughout the organism.

Initially the voices from the physical body are louder than those from the Spirit. Those with little understanding or desire to change will rarely achieve victory over their fleshly desires.

But be assured the Holy Spirit can be trusted for victory.

The mind will send images of distress that the body will manifest in pain and discomfort in hopes that the organism will return to its habitual patterns of eating. These are certain signs that the battle is being won and victory is certain, if one stays the course.

Your biggest fears are only as real as your attachment to them. The revelations of Christ that you experience will be the fuel that will separate you from the influences and attachments of this physical world.

The devil hates those who are willing to sacrifice their bodies on the altar of self-death and make the commitment to trust God for their deliverance. There are special angels assigned to those whose determination and will are submitted to the Father.

I have had first-hand experience in these matters and know what I am speaking about. But don't just take my word for it. Discover the truth of these things for yourself.

SECTION VI

THE BODY

Some Pharisees asked Jesus when the Kingdom of God would come. His answer was, "The Kingdom of God does not come in such a way as to be seen.

No one will say, 'Look, here it is!' or, 'There it is!'; because the Kingdom of God is within you."

Luke 17: 20-21 TEV

The Kingdom of God cannot be found in a city or church. According to Jesus, it resides inside those who are IN CHRIST. In order to understand this, it is required for us to clean our physical body for His residence. This is accomplished expressly through fasting. There are no short cuts, and it does not matter the amount of scripture we know or quote. Those who do not fast will find it difficult to maintain a dwelling place for His presence.

Many Christians feel the presence of the Holy Spirit on occasions, which may be described as the "anointing." But those who maintain a lifestyle of fasting are more likely to enjoy His habitation inside their spirit.

The body and soul must be reconnected to the Spirit in man to live in true order and experience the reality of the Kingdom of God. True prosperity and fulfillment begins the instant we are truly born "into" Christ.

Dear friend, I know that you are spiritually well. I pray that you're doing well in every other way and that you're healthy.

3 John 2 GW

Beloved, I pray that you may prosper in all things and be healthy, even as your soul prospers.

3 John 2 WEB

Our body is the temple of God and, as such, we are responsible to maintain this amazing instrument to live in health, both physically and spiritually, while fulfilling our destiny on earth.

Previously, we explained the role of the Holy Spirit as the guardian of God's blood in the earth. The Holy Spirit is the designated person of the Godhead assigned to empower God's people with His wisdom and power.

The infilling of His Spirit is the supernatural power designed to change us from a life of consumption to a life of giving. The first man chose to consume instead of give. God asked for one thing in the Garden. Nevertheless, the man rejected his request and chose to eat from the very thing God warned him against. The Bible says God so loved that He gave. Those who have chosen to enter God's kingdom must do it by giving God their lives. If one changes their priority from consuming to giving, fasting will become a lifestyle.

The body is the center of attention for most of society, because it is the source of physical gratification. The statement Jesus makes in the following scripture defines the priority between the natural and spiritual dimension.

So I say to you, **Take no thought** *for your life, about food or drink, or about clothing for your body. Is not life more than food, and the body more than its clothing?*

Matthew 6:25 BBE

Jesus is separating the life of the physical body from that of the spirit. He appears to be saying our thoughts are what determine the value we place on the physical or spiritual world. Later in the chapter, He explains that His Father takes care of those whose thoughts are about Him and not earthly things.

Whose end is perdition, whose god is the belly, and whose glory is in their shame, who mind earthly things.

Philippians 3:19 ASV

Societies whose appetites are their god will never find satisfaction, but will always be searching. That is a recipe for physical, mental and spiritual problems. Moreover, it will reproduce future generations with the same characteristics. The kingdoms of this world—including religion—have no solution for problems originating from the spirit of man.

God sent the perfect sacrifice for man to live in divine health.

Those who are overweight and slaves to unhealthy appetites are deceived, but not forsaken or unloved by God. Fasting is the tool designed by God to set you free from the attachments of the physical world, including food. The original design of the body was created to live for thousands of years free from disease.

*My dear friend, I pray that you may in all respects prosper and **enjoy good health, just as your soul already prospers.***

3 John 2 Weymouth

CHAPTER 15

FASTING IS MEDICINE

Fasting is God's natural detoxification treatment for those with medical conditions and is considerably better than destroying the body with prescription drugs. Fasting is medicine, and it has no side effects. Medical science has reported results supporting fasting as a preventive measure that increases overall health, vitality and resistance to disease.

When properly utilized, fasting can be a powerful tool in helping your body do what it does best...heal itself. It is the answer to a surprising number of questions.[1]

Fasting is the best method one can use to repair the physical body, including the organs and cells.[2] Dr. Benjamin Horne believes that fasting could one day be prescribed as a treatment for preventing diabetes and coronary heart disease.

---

[1] Alan Goldhamer, D.C. and Jennifer Marano, D.C. "Fasting Is the Answer. What is the Question?" Health Science, Spring 2011.

[2] Intermountain Medical Center. "Routine periodic fasting is good for your health, and your heart, study suggests." Science Daily, 3 Apr. 2011. Web. 24 Nov. 2011.

In addition, fasting is even recognized by science to purify and cleanse the organs. The digestive tract requires the most immune system support because it is the part of the body most exposed to bacteria, viruses, parasites and toxins. After food travels through the intestines, it enters the blood to the liver, the largest natural detoxification system of the body.

The liver dissolves and removes the toxic waste produced through digestion, including the organic and the chemical pollutants now present in the food supply. Fasting allows the liver and immune system the freedom to use healthy blood to reenergize and vitalize all the organs in the body.

One of the most important physiological aspects of fasting is the internal energy formerly used to digest food is now harnessed to clean and heal the organism. The principle behind that is simple. When the intake of food is temporarily stopped, many systems of the body are given a break from the hard work of digestion. The extra energy allows the body the chance to heal and restore itself.

In addition, the body will burn stored calories as fuel to eliminate toxic substances stored in the organs. During the absence of food, the body will systematically cleanse itself of everything except vital tissue.

Many physiological changes occur in the body during fasting. During the first day or so, the body uses its glycogen reserves, or sugars, which supply the basic energy of the body. After these are depleted, the body begins using stored fat.

The brain requires complex sugars or glucose to function most effectively. In fact, Dr. Norberto Coimbra's studies show that the brain requires twice as much energy or glucose than any other cells in the body. In addition, his research found that mental concentration actually drains glucose from a key part of the brain associated with memory and learning—underscoring just how crucial this blood sugar is for proper brain function.[3]

To obtain sufficient amounts of glucose for the brain, the body begins to break down muscle tissue during the second day of the fast. Although protein is being used by the body during the fast, a person fasting 40 days on water will not suffer a deficiency of protein, vitamins, minerals or fatty acids.

In order to fuel the brain, the body would need to burn over a pound of muscle a day, but the body has developed another way to create energy that saves important muscle mass. This protein-sparing process is called ketosis, which occurs during the third day of a fast for men and the second day for women. The liver converts stored fat and other nonessential tissues into amino acids called ketones, which can be used by the brain, muscles, and heart as energy.

According to A. J. Carlson, Professor of Physiology, University of Chicago, a healthy, well-nourished man can live from 50 to 75 days without food, provided he is not exposed to harsh elements or emotional stress.

---

[3] Dr. Norberto Cysne Coimbra, Ph.D. "Thermoeffector neuronal pathways in fever: a study in rats showing a new role of the locus coeruleus", Faculty of Medicine of Riberirao Preto, 1998. http://www.fi.edu/learn/brain/carbs.html

The healthy cells remain perfectly sound even if they are reduced in size and strength for a time.[4] The benefits of fasting are more than losing weight or healing chronic conditions. Fasting releases power that transcends the physical world. Nevertheless, without the Holy Sprit's presence, fasting is just another self-help tool for those who want to look good and lose weight.

The physical body is a magnificent machine designed to transform matter into energy in order for man to discover the wonders of his creator. For example, if someone eats an apple, the stomach starts the process of digestion until the matter (consumed food) becomes chemical compounds and acids small enough to enter the blood stream. It is this transition from matter to energy that supplies both the physical and psychological needs of man.

Physical food is chemically altered through digestion in order to supply the necessities for both body and soul. The energy exchange from the food to the blood is the first step in understanding the mystery of God's design.

Research indicates that white blood cells increase during prolonged fasting, producing a healthy environment for cell reproduction.[5] In addition, blood acts as the body's spiritual antibiotic. If it were not continually working to digest food, it could offer healing properties to diseased organs.

---

[4] Ron Laqerquist, "Fasting vs. Starvation", http://www.freedomyou.com/fasting_book/Fasting%20_vs_ starvation.htm

[5] T.C. Fry's Life Science Health System, http://www.rawfoodexplained.com/introduction-to-fasting/what-the-body-does-when-you-fast.html

God tells Moses in Leviticus the importance of blood.

For the life of the flesh is in the blood, and I have given it to you upon the altar to make atonement for your souls; for it is the blood that makes atonement for the soul.

Leviticus 17:11 NKJV

I believe the Holy Spirit is assigned to bring souls back to God through Christ and uses the spiritual properties inherent in the blood as His conduit.

Why? Because we have learned that the blood was designed by God to supply both physical life and spiritual DNA. The devil knows the power of blood, because it is what defeated him. I believe that God required the Israelites to eat certain foods to protect their blood as well as to provide proper nutrition.

Science spends billions of dollars on drugs to prevent the spread of disease, but hardly anything is spent to educate the world about the need to fast.

Isn't it about time the Body of Christ rises up and leads the world instead of following it?

CHAPTER 16

FASTING AND PHYSIOLOGY

Capitalism, particularly in the United States, produces insatiable consumers whose desires are their gods. People who spend their money and resources on material goods determine the economic prosperity of the world. The more they consume, the greater the demand for expansion both physically and mentally.

One of the side effects of capitalism is the fast food industry. These are restaurants that prepare foods quickly to satisfy hunger but offer little in the way of nutrition. The menus in those restaurants consist primarily of processed meats and fried foods, which have been linked to sickness and disease.

Nutritional factors can have a significant impact on brain function, which can result in numerous mental aberrations, such as depression, anxiety, attention deficit hyperactivity, schizophrenia, autism, bulimia, anorexia and bi-polar disorders, to name a few. Bad diets and wrong eating habits combined with the "love" of money is a primary cause for illness.

Thoughts and their origin are as mysterious as the universes and galaxies. Nevertheless, science has discovered the association between the foods we eat and our mental activity. In order to maintain self-control, will power and the ability to think clearly, the brain needs nutrients. The craving for unhealthy food is the by-product of a body whose mind has been chemically altered with wrong eating.[6]

Many scientists believe that fast food is not only unhealthy but also has addictive qualities. There is evidence that shows fast-food consumption reinforces the desire for more of the same empty calories. Most people complain about being unable to stop craving the unhealthy food even though they know it is killing them.[7]

Research reveals the effects fast food has on the brain from the hormones, such as leptin and galanin. The latest findings indicate that fast food increases leptin and decreases galanin, which creates a malfunction in the brain called "hypothalamic-obesity". This is why overweight individuals continue to eat because their bodies cannot tell when they have eaten enough.[8]

Linus Pauling Ph.D., a two-time Nobel Prize winner, said, "It is now recognized by leading workers in the field that behavior is determined by the functioning of the brain, and that the

---

[6] Jeff Thiboutot BS, CN, CPT. Food, Mind, And Mood: The Connection Between What People Eat and How They Feel and Act Posted: Aug 14, 2008.

[7] Paul M Johnson & Paul J Kenny, "Dopamine D2 receptors in addiction-like reward dysfunction and compulsive eating in obese rats," Nature Neuroscienc.13, pp. 635–641 February 2010.

[8] Leibowitz SF, Kim T (1992) Impact of a galanin antagonist on exogenous galanin and natural patterns of fat ingestion. Brain Res 599:148–152.

functioning of the brain is dependent on its composition and structure."[9] The brain produces chemicals called neurotransmitters that regulate our moods, emotions and even the way we experience pain. Nutrients in the foods we eat trigger certain amino acids that, in turn, produce or decrease production of chemicals such as dopamine, epinephrine and serotonin. People who display symptoms of fatigue, weight problems and short attention spans are generally deficient in these amino acids. The inability to concentrate and focus is one of the biggest obstacles to education and hearing the Spirit of God.

Sadly those who display these symptoms or feel ill most likely go to a physician who generally prescribes a pharmaceutical drug to treat the symptoms. The drug may alleviate the symptoms, but in time it will make other organs vulnerable by lowering the body's natural resistance to diseases.

Another overwhelming reason why people, even Christians, suffer from health conditions is sin. I know many Christians whose lifestyle of wrong eating was challenged by the Holy Spirit, but their refusal to obey has led to illness.

All disobedience is sin, and this type of disobedience is often characterized by the combination of surfeiting and eating "junk" foods. The word surfeiting means overeating or gluttony, and it is one of the root causes for illness in society, both physically and spiritually.

---

[9] David Perlmutter, MD, FACN and Carol Colman, "Raise a Smarter Child by Kindergarten" Broadway Books, 2006

But take heed to yourselves, lest haply your hearts be overcharged with surfeiting, and drunkenness, and cares of this life, and that day come on you suddenly as a snare:

Luke 21: 34 ASV

The physical matter used to form the body is the same material it needs to maintain it most efficiently, which is why consuming processed foods destroys the organism.

For example, if you were to put diesel fuel in a car that operates on gas, the engine would not work. Therefore, if one consumes sugary soft drinks and foods prepared from non-organic materials, the organs will fail.

Fasting will reduce or even heal nearly every chronic condition, including allergies, anxiety, arthritis, asthma, depression, diabetes, headaches, heart disease, high cholesterol, low blood sugar, digestive disorders, mental illness, and obesity.[10]

Food is often used to control the emotions. But if the food is not healthy, it will inhibit the production of serotonin. Eating sugar or too many carbohydrates is a quick fix for the chemical imbalance but produces long-term health problems such as diabetes or high blood pressure.

Those who depend on doctors to solve their health problems have not understood the power of the cross.

---

[10] Dr. Ben Kim, "Fasting For Health," A Spiritually Enlightening Online Magazine. January Volume 8 Issue 2 ISSN# 1708-3265.

The book Pharmakeia by my wife, Ana Méndez Ferrell, describes in great detail the atrocities committed by the pharmaceutical industry in conjunction with the health system.

According to information from a statistical study of hospital deaths in the U.S., which was conducted at the University of Toronto, pharmaceutical drugs kill more people every year than are killed in traffic accidents.[11]

The study shows that more than two million American-hospitalized patients suffered a serious adverse drug reaction (ADR) within the 12-month period of the study. The study found that over 100,000 died. The researchers found that over 75 per cent of these ADRs were dose-dependent, which suggests they were due to the inherent toxicity of the drugs rather than to allergic reactions.

The data did not include fatal reactions caused by accidental overdoses or errors in administration of the drugs. If these had been included, it is estimated that another 100,000 deaths would be added to the total every year.

---

[11] Guylaine Lanctôt. "The Medical Mafia," Vesica Piscis, 2002, page. 258.

CHAPTER 17

PERSONAL EXPERIENCES OF FASTING

The first time someone said they were fasting, I honestly did not know what they were talking about. After it was explained to me, I thought it was interesting and challenging, but not necessarily for me. Boy, was I in for a shock.

In the days following that conversation, the Holy Spirit reminded me constantly about the subject of fasting. Moreover, everywhere I turned, fasting was the topic of discussion. I was reluctant to study the scriptures at first, because I knew what I would find, namely a command to fast.

My preoccupation with this word created many sleepless nights and endless questions. What was fasting and was it really that important? The churches I attended rarely spoke on the subject and most of the people in the congregations did not appear to miss many meals.

I was particularly shocked to find research that indicated obesity to be the number one health issue facing Americans. I then discovered that "church members" tend to be more overweight than the general population. And according to a study the Southern Baptists, have the distinction of being the most overweight of the religious groups studied.[12]

The preparation for my first fast began several days before starting with reducing the intake of all meat and fried foods. The following three days my diet consisted of vegetables, cooked and raw. The final day of preparation I only ate fruits.

My first complete fast consisted only of water and lasted for three days. Although it was not very long, it changed me. The physical change was not as significant as the joy I felt for having pleased the Lord.

My first attempts at fasting were dismal failures. The primary objective for fasting is to concentrate on the Lord. Sadly, all I could do was think about eating.

For those of you who have had similar experiences, take heart. The Holy Spirit helps those who persevere. It was not long before my obsession for food subsided and the peace of God filled my mind and heart.

Subsequently, I learned to drink a large glass of salty hot water and soak in a tub of hot water, while listening to worship music. This served several purposes, but mainly it purged my bladder and intestines, kept me relaxed and helped me stay focused on

---

[12] Wendy Ashley, "Obesity in the Body of Christ," Southern Baptist Convention, Executive Committee, SBC LIFE (ISSN 1081-8189), Volume 20, Number 1, © 2011.

the Holy Spirit. Later I discovered that my body stopped craving food after three or four days, and the biggest battle from that point forward was with my thoughts.

During my first attempts, I would succumb to temptations and had to begin again after overcoming remorse and guilt. The Holy Spirit gently encouraged me to start over and not listen to the voices of condemnation from the devil.

Those early experiences planted seeds inside my soul that have produced patience and endurance for the things of the Spirit. The small steps I made in the beginning have helped me to become an overcomer.

By your steadfastness and patient endurance you shall win the true life of your souls.

Luke 21:19 AMP

Fasting taught me, among other things, that food is as addictive as drugs. So I determined to be conscious of each time my mouth opened to eat. I had to ask myself if the material going inside me was for His glory or my satisfaction.

After several smaller fasts, the first of what became many 40-day fasts had arrived. Initially the number of days made me a bit anxious, but when I remembered my angelic visitations, my determination returned.

Each day began with worship and quiet meditation. My job allowed me to work from my home most weeks. The days that required travel I would spend listening to teachings or worship music in the car. On many occasions I would take clients to lunch or dinner and explain to some of them that I was fasting.

Many of my customers were surprised that someone would voluntarily go without food, while others seemed supportive. The vast majority were interested but expressed no interest in pursuing that lifestyle.

As the days and weeks went by, so did the intensity of the experiences with the Holy Spirit. One evening the presence of the Lord became so strong that I fell to the floor and wept uncontrollably. I lost all awareness of time but my mind and body felt waves of ecstasies and terror simultaneously. I learned later that the Lord was preparing me for His habitation.

The Holy Spirit asked me how much of Him I wanted, and I knew my answer would determine the level of physical and mental annihilation required to accomplish His work.

My response was to fill me. Almost immediately, it was as if my body was plugged into a 220-volt outlet. The feeling of electrical waves changed to tsunamis, but it was never more than I could endure.

Moreover, He told me that in order to know Jesus and His Glory, I must become spiritually hungry. I did not understand what He meant at the time. So I began to cry out, "Show me your way,

Lord." Then it happened! My desperate cry for more of Him developed a spiritual hunger that replaced all of my natural appetites. In other words, if the Holy Spirit can make you spiritually hungry, you will lose your natural desire for the things of this world, including food.

My soul and body were being transformed, and the appetites of this world seemed meaningless and unappealing. My desire to fellowship with the Father made me hungry. It occurred to me that this is why Jesus separated Himself to feed on His Father's presence.

The following day was the beginning of my second week and my energy level was noticeably higher. My body and mind experienced levels of sensitivity that reminded me of my youth. I remember going outside that morning and jumping on my son's trampoline. The thought of doing that the previous week would have made me nauseous.

The following day after spending the afternoon in prayer I felt the fire of God touch me from the inside out. Each sensation created more hunger inside my soul and a deeper longing for Christ. The visits and experiences were only limited by doubt and unbelief within my mind.

The fire increased, and the physical pains were at times unbearable. But something incredible occurred through my spiritual hunger. A physical and mental shield seemed to envelope me from any more unbelief. The enemy used mental images, wrong choices and bad decisions from the past as a mental wedge between the Holy Spirit and myself.

Nevertheless, the spiritual hunger from my desire for more of Him created a knowing inside my spirit of forgiveness and victory. The overwhelming power of love flooded my soul and erased the unbelief. That experience marked me for the remainder of my fast. I believe Jesus baptized me in His fire during those encounters. The experience lasted all night and into the following day.

The following week I sensed the presence of angels in my room. It was on that occasion that I remember tasting the liquid I saw years ago. During that time, an angel was holding a container whose appearance could only be described as "liquid light." The angel indicated that I could taste the contents in the jar if I would fast 40 days.

I remember trembling as the waves of His Glory filled me from the inside out. I was unable to determine if I was in my body or out. Time stood still and the ceiling in the room opened to a bright light filled with faces and clouds. During that time, my awareness of the invisible world and eternity changed forever.

Each day the Holy Spirit would visit me with an incomprehensible sense of love and encouragement. One evening He showed me the nature of creation and its origin from the mind of God. I witnessed the structure of faith and why it was the only substance that pleased God. I understood everything He was saying through my spirit, but in my mind it sounded like a foreign language.

My spiritual hunger increased until my natural appetites ceased to have any control over my physical body. My spirit was gaining dominance over my mind and body.

The following day started the final week of my first 40-day fast. That morning I remember sensing that my life no longer belonged to me, that somehow my experiences had ushered in a new level of sonship with my Father. The freedom I was experiencing could not be described by words. Then I understood the words of Jesus in John.

If the Son sets you free, then you will be really free.

John 8:36 NET

Then the Holy Spirit commanded me to start reading the Bible from cover to cover. This began the most amazing journey of my life. From Genesis to Revelation the words and experiences came alive. The book became an open door into the mind of the Holy Spirit.

The power of those words fed my spirit and changed my mind. The Holy Spirit was transforming me through the living Word. I experienced the scriptures coming to life and introducing me to Christ in a way I had never experienced before. I believe my birth into His kingdom started during those 40 days.

Fasting is a small step relative to the amazing adventures of eternity waiting for those who love Him. Those willing to persevere will be rewarded if they keep their eyes focused on the person who sacrificed everything.

CHAPTER 18

FASTING BIRTHS PROPHETS

My life as a prophet was born from worship and fasting. Worship became not only music but also the harmony between my spirit and His. The resonation of my heart and mind had to be changed into the frequency of heaven in order to understand His ways.

Fasting was the vehicle the Lord has used to change me into an instrument He can use. The process has been amazing, and the results are a perpetual fountain flowing inside my spirit.

One day after fasting solid food for several weeks, I recall feelings of joy beginning to sweep through my soul like a roaring wind. Laughter bubbled up like a fountain, and all at once something remarkable happened inside my mind.

My thoughts changed from pictures with recognizable shapes and sizes to waves of color. The waves then transformed from color to physical objects such as a chair, table or person. I did not understand what was happening but remained calm.

During the evening while I was worshiping, the room filled with what appeared to be clouds. There were many of them, and each appeared to have their own special characteristics. The sound of my worship changed the shapes and sizes of the clouds, and at one point they joined together to form what appeared to be a ladder. I looked up the ladder and witnessed angels and saints moving between two dimensions. Immediately, I was reminded of what Jesus told Nathaniel.

Nathanael said to him, "How do you know me?" Jesus answered and said to him, "Before Philip called you, I saw you under the fig tree."

Nathanael answered him, "Rabbi, you are the Son of God; you are the King of Israel."

Jesus answered and said to him, "Do you believe because I told you that I saw you under the fig tree? You will see greater things than this."

And he said to him, "Amen, amen, I say to you, you will see the sky opened and the angels of God ascending and descending on the Son of Man."

John 1:48-51 NAB

That experience opened my understanding to the prophetic realm. Later the Holy Spirit trained me to trust His ways regardless of the methods He used.

For example, I would associate a certain smell with a person or place and within a matter of hours or days the person or place would be right before my eyes in the natural. At first I believed it to be a coincidence until the experience repeated itself over and over again.

Before long, it was commonplace to know things before they actually happened in time. Most people consider this to be a common occurrence for prophets, but I can assure you that nothing the Holy Spirit does is common.

After being baptized in the Holy Spirit, my sensitivity to the invisible world became increasingly more intense. God's kingdom is eternal and timeless. Therefore, it is limited with physical words, which makes it difficult to explain to those unfamiliar with a lifestyle of fasting.

My thirst for deeper and greater experiences in the Lord propelled me to longer periods of fasting and more intense times of prayer. During these times, my understanding was expanded through experiences in the spiritual world and so too were my interactions outside of time and space.

The most striking difference separating the two dimensions appeared to be a curtain-like fabric that resembled a waterfall of light. The light sounded like water falling, but the closer I moved towards the veil the quieter it became. Furthermore, the light changed colors and sound relative to position of my viewpoint.

There were no shadows or darkness, which indicated an absence of time and movement. Any attempt to describe the circumstance or rationalize the events altered my perception or memory of the occurrence. Quickly, I heard the Holy Spirit tell me to be still and not to think with my mind, but understand with my spirit.

I later learned that my mind was interfering with the spiritual dimension of God because His realm is timeless. Therefore, any thoughts arising from the temporal world contained doubt or fear and prevented any further connection to His realms of glory.

This experience made me understand many things, one being the speed of thoughts. It was clear the images from my mind hindered the ability of the Holy Spirit to display the wonders of the invisible world. My perceptions of "things" outside the physical world were constructed from thoughts and images that restricted comprehension.

Later the Holy Spirit explained to me that the world and everything material was God's idea before it became physical. The material world requires both visible and invisible elements to sustain it. Light and time are two of the consistent factors in maintaining the integrity and continuity of physical life.

Science uses light as an important variable in its equation for determining the relativity of matter. Research is being conducted today in the hopes of discovering the "origin" of the universe by colliding electrons together at the speed of light. The anti-matter that is collected from these collisions is expected to provide clues to the source of energy, which to date is unknown.

God formed everything from His thoughts, which resonated in His command for light to become visible (Genesis 1:3). The light God released is the light of the life of all men. His light is described on the mountain of transfiguration, which is much different from the light of this world.

Jesus is the physical manifestation of God's words. The Word of God was manifested to destroy the darkness that kept men separated from God, called sin. Today His Word sustains both the invisible and visible world.

It has been critical for my faith to understand His authority and power over both the seen and unseen world. Man is equipped to understand both physical and spiritual realms, if he will recognize the "living Word" as Christ.

It is obvious to me that the invisible world is the substance of God, and the material world is the manifestation of God through Christ.

All things came into being through Him, and apart from Him nothing that exists came into being.

John 1:3 Weymouth

That revelation changed my perception of the world and increased my awareness of the strategies of the enemy through our thoughts. Most importantly, I discovered my thoughts could be changed through extended periods of fasting. In fact, the title of this book was born from that understanding.

The longer I fasted, the sooner I began to realize the real battle was not doing without food but bringing my thoughts under submission. I had read the scripture in 2 Corinthians before, but until then it was not revelation.

*For though we may be **living in the flesh,** we are not fighting after the way of the flesh*

(For the arms with which we are fighting are not those of the flesh, but are strong before God for the destruction of high places);

*Putting an end to reasonings, and every high thing, which is lifted up against the knowledge of God, and **causing every thought to come under the authority of Christ;***

*Being ready to give punishment to whatever is against his authority, **after you have made it clear that you are completely under his control.***

2 Corinthians 10:3-6 BBE

Furthermore, the more I fasted, the easier it was for me to yield to His instructions and surrender to His authority.

Every thought that exalts desires or wants above submission is out of order and must be submitted to Christ. Otherwise, they become spiritual roadblocks to our righteousness, peace and joy in the Holy Spirit.

Nutritionists are learning that foods are not just protein and carbohydrates but physical matter that influence our thoughts. Some studies indicate these basic nutrients, despite the fact they are similar in calories, vibrate at different frequencies.[13]

Atoms are frequencies of energy that operate in the visible and invisible realms. The speed or vibrations of these atoms create the magnetic attraction that makes up material molecular structures.

Taking this a step further, at the atomic level, the vibrating, energetic, charged particles of food interact to a significant degree with the blood and cells. These vibrations affect the molecular structure of our mind and body.

Understanding the basis of frequencies and vibrations can helps us understand that the world considered real is actually vibrating so fast it appears to be solid. All atoms vibrate at different frequency rates, depending on their complexity and density.

In other words, our physical world consists of material from the invisible realm. The spiritual world is invisible to our naked eye because of the speed in which it moves.

---

[13] Jakob Böhme, "God's handiwork: The Doctrine of Signatures," Idaho Observe, Ingri Cassel, July 2008.

Science measures the atomic structures separating the two worlds with sophisticated equipment. The instruments reveal the frequency and vibrations of the spinning atoms that form our material world. Fasting speeds up the atomic structure inside persons who reduce the amount of matter they eat and increase the amount of time they spend in prayer.

I believe satan was interested in the physical body of Moses because of the physical transformation that happened to him from his supernatural experiences in God's presence.

Moses was 120 years old when he died. His eyesight never became poor, and he never lost his physical strength.

Deuteronomy 34:7 GW

Not even the chief angel Michael did this. In his quarrel with the Devil, when they argued about who would have the body of Moses, Michael did not dare condemn the Devil with insulting words, but said, "The Lord rebuke you!"

Jude 9 TEV

Hitler, was said to have searched the world looking for the spear that penetrated the side of Jesus. Why? Because the demons inside him know the blood of Christ is immortal and eternal. All of hell knows that and recognizes those who carry His DNA in their spirits.[14]

---

[14] Mark Harris 1996, "Further Reading: The Spear of Destiny," Trevor Ravenscroft, Published by Neville Spearman, London, 1974.

L. Emerson Ferrell

My experience in the spiritual realm through fasting has produced physiological changes in my body including increased stamina and attention span. At the writing of this book I am 62 and do not wear eyeglasses or take medications, including aspirin.

If our spirit remains in contact with the Holy Spirit, the physical body will be dramatically affected.

Fasting will increase the presence of God. The presence of God changes the electromagnetic field of the physical body. This results in attracting heaven's frequency and revelation of Christ. That experience will create a hunger inside your soul that natural food will never be able to satisfy.

THE END

191

CONCLUSION

It is not my desire or goal to change those who oppose my revelation of truth. The truth will eventually prevail after those who oppose it die out and a new generation arises familiar with not only the revelation God has given to me but also fresh revelation.

The value of a prophet is measured by the revelation of Christ they carry. If His voice is not heard, the prophet has not done their job. Jesus never tried to force the religious people to change their minds. He brought the revelation of His Father and completed the Law.

The Lord has allowed me these adventures through fasting to see the reality of the invisible realm. The spirit realm is the source of all reality, and it is interacting with the physical world constantly.

Christians should be solving problems in the world because of their connection with Christ. Sadly, that is not the case. I believe more and more people are becoming disillusioned with the status quo. My hope this book will help awaken those who have been dissatisfied with the answers they have received from religious leaders.

My journey has just begun, and yours will begin as well once you choose a lifestyle of fasting. Our world supplies opportunities for greater experiences in the unknown realms. Most assuredly, the Holy Spirit will never forsake those whose desire is to discover their origin in God.

If you are reading this book, it is because the precious Holy Spirit has heard your prayers. He knows what you need and has already provided your solutions. But are you willing to change the way you think and feel?

My response to that question changed my life and allowed me to become personal friends with the Holy Spirit. Fasting is one of the many radical sacrifices necessary for this eternal relationship to prosper.

The authority and power began for Jesus after the Holy Spirit led Him into a 40-day fast. Why should it be any different for anyone who wants to follow Him?

Fear prevents most people from making the necessary changes in their lives. The majority of human beings have experienced the voices of fear reminding them of past failures. If you do not remember anything else today, remember this:

Life is filled with failures, but one victory, regardless of how small, will create a new tomorrow for your life

today.

Make fasting a part of your foundation for success, and the devil will flee from you. The visible world was formed from the invisible. Therefore, those whose source of nourishment is spiritual will rule and reign over the material realm.

When you make the sacrifice to fast, the Holy Spirit will activate heaven on your behalf. If you have longed to interact with the angels, fasting will remove the veil and expose you to their participation in your life.

Recommended books
L. Emerson Ferrell

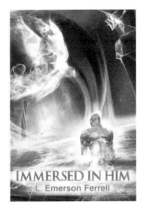

Immersed in Him

Supernatural Believing
Christ Conscious

Becoming the Master's Key